CW00517156

the weira roias

everyday poems from the anthropocene

- Read intro

- Morton bit as well

- Dark Ecology

- Species / spaces ? → defamiliarizing

the weird folds

everyday poems from the anthropocene

Edited by
Maria Sledmere and
Rhian Williams

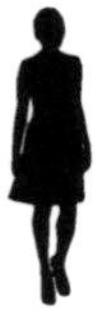

Dostoyevsky Wannabe Originals
An Imprint of Dostoyevsky Wannabe

First Published in 2020
by Dostoyevsky Wannabe Originals
All rights reserved
© All copyright reverts to individual authors

Dostoyevsky Wannabe Originals is an imprint of
Dostoyevsky Wannabe publishing.

www.dostoyevskywannabe.com

This book is a work of fiction. The names, characters and incidents
portrayed in it are the work of the authors' imagination. Any resemblance
to actual persons, living or dead, events or localities is entirely coincidental.

Cover design by Dostoyevsky Wannabe Design

ISBN-978-1-8380156-1-9

No parts of this publication may be reproduced, stored in a retrieval
system, or transmitted in any form or by any means, electronic,
mechanical, photocopying, recording, or otherwise, without the prior
written permission of the copyright owner.

Contents

Part Three

Biographies   279

They all fly away at once, it's spring
Or something, a new season called WHOOSH

Bernadette Mayer

To stay alive one needs a tongue, more than ever.
                    Parts one says:
Here's a little hit from the anthology. Keep one
                    abounce.

Alice Notley

Introduction by
Maria Sledmere and
Rhian Williams

the weird folds: everyday poems from the anthropocene

There is a sentence in French novelist Marie Ndiaye's *Ladivine* (2013) in which exquisite clauses and cadences cleave together differing responses to witnessing an unprecedented shift in a human's relationship with its environment, its context, and the 'more than human'. Calm recognition curls around to protect raw anguish:

> She didn't dare admit it, but she was also afraid Marko would end up spotting the dog, and she delicately squeezed his hand and spoke any words that came to mind to keep Marko's attention on her, his daughter Annika, who, though only eight, thought herself seasoned enough to calmly accept that her mother had chosen to look after them from inside the skin of a dog on the Droysenstrasse's icy sidewalk, whereas her father, she thought, her poor distraught father, should he ever realize such a thing, could never accept it without even more grief than he already felt (p. 225).

It is one of many slippages in Ndiaye's writing, glitches and metamorphoses (in 1989 she published, *La Femme changée en bûche* – The lady changes into a log) that disarm empiricist accounts of the relations between body and mind, human and more than human, nature and culture; NDiaye explains, 'My only way to see the abstract things is to embody them.' And yet, NDiaye explains, 'My subjects are not major issues, but ordinary stories, banal' (Bady 2016).

When we began thinking about this anthology of 'anthropocene poetry', we were simultaneously thinking about – because we were living in – the 'everyday': the category of experience that Rita Felski defines so compellingly as 'the blurred speck at the edge of one's vision that disappears when looked at directly' (2000, p. 15). The 'everyday' (the ordinary? the banal?), despite its elusiveness – its evasion of critical gaze – is the plane on which our experience of climate change manifests. In the waking up each day, the routines, the food, the drinks, the washing, the cleaning, the caring for pets, the tending to the body, the maintenance of the flesh with which we thrive as mammals, is adumbrated our relationship to the earth; our status as 'climate subjects' is constellated in our daily encounters and intertwinings with other beings, with objects, with materials, with the spores and detritus of life lived. And yet the everyday's very ubiquity – its inevitability – renders it overwhelming, even invisible, in its data scale; one feels there is just too much 'everyday' to be captured and therefore to be seen. It is a weird kind of air we must breathe.

The Anthropocene, it occurred to us, was both entirely different and entirely similar to this quotidian phenomenon. Proposed in around 2000 by atmospheric chemist Paul J.Crutzen and biologist Eugene F. Stoermer, 'Anthropocene'

names a new geological epoch during which human activity
– most prominently industrial fossil fuel extraction and the
production of infinitely durable petrochemical materials – is
'considered to be the dominant influence on the environment,
climate, and ecology of the earth' (*OED*). Yet the controver-
sies it immediately courted, even at the moment of its being
proposed (could an Anthropocene of some 250 years duration
be geologically meaningful, is it discernible in a discipline
that works in numbers of millions of years?) illustrates vividly
how the idea, like that of the 'everyday', poses a problem of
scale. If, for some geologists, the Anthropocene is too small
in its scale – not yet ripe for geological tools of measurement
– for most humans, its span is too wide, its significance not
bearable. The proposal that human activity is now materially
determining the constituent parts of the earth disorientates us,
tips our compass points: the soil we stand on did not exist in
this way before we did. The earth is not host but offspring, not
background but consequence. Culture has bored into nature;
nature has become culture. Where are our categories now?

For Kathryn Yusoff, the disorientation such a realisation
generates is itself a symptom, a fatal weakness borne of taxo-
nomic violence. White geology (the discipline that maintains
the model of geological epochs in the first place), she tells us –
in its abstractions, its extractions, and its theories, particularly
'the language of materiality and its division between life and
nonlife' (2018, p. 9) – denies the bodies (specifically black and

brown bodies) that were (or are) its very lifeforce (or sacrifice). Asking, 'how is geology as a discipline and extraction process cooked together in the crucible of slavery and colonialism?' (ibid.), Yusoff's work sounds out the fractures and fissures – the power relations, the privileges, and the repressions – that lattice accounts of our earth, its histories and its present catastrophes. Understanding the Anthropocene not as an objective category – a geological age – but as a *genre* (2018, p. 6), and, radically for her discipline, taking her cue from the Martinique poets, Aimé Césaire and Édouard Glissant, Yusoff compels us to think about the cultural forms that the idea of an Anthropocene generates, to be attentive to the writing modes we employ when we write about the earth and to meditate on their determining effects, to 'intrude' on the '*givenness* of geology as an innocent or natural description of the world' (p. 10). Not standing over – categorising, objectifying – but deeply within, and constituent of, the minerality of our planet, Yusoff's 'alluvial subjectivities' walk out to disarm the very critical apparatus that sought to tame them. We found this inspirational.

Such inspiration is needed more than ever. Writing in March 2020, in the midst of a government lockdown in response to the Covid-19 crisis, the parameters of the 'everyday' become all the more pressurised. As many of us begin working from home, schooling from home and socialising from home, domestic space and daily rhythms are pushed to the forefront of how we define being, relationality, desire and survival in a moment of genuine pandemic. Covid-19 is viral to the core: both in its highly contagious RNA transmission and in the warping, rapid spread of information, memes, news and cultural responses that it seamlessly invites in our post-internet age. One critique of the Anthropocene, taken as an epochal term, is its tendency to universalise 'Man'. The coronavirus pandemic is an accelerated example of how unequal the distribution of global and planetary harms and responsibilities are, dependent on economic, infrastructural, gendered, racialised and class differences—to name but a few. Donna Haraway's proposed alternative term 'Chthulucene' captures the myriad entangled stories and lives that make up our 'thick present'; it means both staying with 'the trouble of living and dying in response-ability on a damaged earth' and also 'a time of beginnings, a time for on-going' (2016, p. 1-2). Haraway suggests that the 'kin stories' of the Chthulucene require 'viral response-abilities', where 'meanings and materials' are carried between beings and times 'in order to infect processes and practices that might yet ignite epidemics of multispecies recuperation and maybe even flourishing' (2016, p. 114). It surely indicates the shifting vectors of our times that Haraway's celebration of epidemic metaphor now seems slightly uncomfortable. What responsibilities do we have in working with language drawn from disciplines of science and anthropology? What contexts define value, accountability and expression in times of crisis? As the present thickens into uncertain futures, we face a sheer kind of *weirdness*.

Sticking with 'anthropocene', we hope to keep open this strange plane of multiple interpretation, to hold to constant account its definition of the human, its fraught, extractive histories. We make a fold in the days, refresh our feed. We decapitalise 'anthropocene' to demonstrate wariness over the totalising authority ascribed to an epochal term, and to recognise its viral agency and mutation within a burgeoning cultural vernacular around climate crisis. Along with Joanna Zylinska, we consider the anthropocene as more of 'a thought device that helps us to visualise the multiple event of extinction' (2016, p. 178), and one that offers a tracery of temporal folds, interventions, mediations and ongoing processes.

The earth as it is experienced now – precarious, shifting, radically reconsidered, imperilled – is inhabited by changed bodies, by altered subjects, by new materialities. And those new materialities are forged in the contradictory and slippery crucible of the digital. Coincident with politicised accounts of the soil and its mineral 'wealth', and with probing and empathetic accounts of our kinship with more than human creatures, objects, and other phenomena, is the emergence of a generation of agents connected by server, data, bytes, memes, gifs, touch screens, and superhighways. As we are ever more aware of ourselves as earth dwellers – intertwined through rhizomatic horizontality – we are also oddly ambient, dema-

more like a genre

16

terialised, drifting in space. Snagged on this contradiction – an electrically charged digital/analogue dyad – we wondered where an anthology could settle. And so we asked poets to generate a poetics of enquiry (wherein the poetic *thinks*) that contends with how shared habitats emerge from and through representation (in art, in culture); we wanted to curate an anthology that begins an archive of the now, that documents the media of contemporaneity as 'a weirdly floating "we" snaps into a blurry focus' (Stewart 2007, p. 27).

The collection that has emerged is, we hope readers will agree, dynamic and disarming, glittering and occult. It is by no means exhaustive – the majority of our poets are UK-based – and we bring it together as a set of questions, provocations or possible directions; it is intended to be generative and cannot be definitive. Its folds proliferate. 'The problem is not how to finish a fold', Gilles Deleuze argues, 'but how to continue it, to have it go through the ceiling, how to bring it to infinity' (1993, p. 34). Our title, *the weird folds*, bears a slippage between verb and noun. Its focus, then, is always in a transitive state, turning over the hours, words and days, the object and action. For Timothy Morton, 'weird' describes the 'twisted, looping form' of ecological awareness (2016, p. 6). What would it mean to loop into a fold, to fold into a loop? We see the fold as a potential moment of expression, a brush against matter, a lyric turn towards and away from presence, the subject(s) speaking. What would it mean, as our title suggests, for the weird to fold, or for those folds to be weird? We believe poetry has a special power to immerse readers in these necessary questions of meaning and experience. Like Jack Spicer, 'I am thinking that a poem could go on forever' (2008).

As we read our submissions, we sensed some overlapping concerns, themes, motifs and approaches — although the collection is characterised as much by its diversity as anything else. We grouped the pieces into three loose 'phases': such an arrangement allowed us to feel for affinities, to create a sense of mood without reducing the openness of each work to categorisation. Each phase is a kind of twisting together of the various pleats of meaning that writers are finding in the anthropocene. Readers will brush against many different forms and genres, from 'classic' lyric to experimental poetics: we offer poems as places where things can come together, be bedfellows or flickering kin. We suggest poetry as a mode where form – page arrangement, convention (and unconvention), figurative language, type and handwriting – allows *things* to be held in new relations. It can tolerate oddness, stimulate energy, reveal where each stress falls. As Sarah Cave writes for this collection, we are 'exhibiting the poem's ability / to comprehend finality as less than final / by calling forth rhythms'.

We see lots of animals — animals of the field, pet companions, and the non-mammalian (ocean-dwelling, insects, birds...); we witness humans 'becoming animal'. We note powerful spirits of curiosity throughout — poking at things, sifting through things, preserving and wandering amongst. Fables and layers of myth. We see acts of noticing, observation and archiving, of incantation, ritual and uprising. We see (and maybe see is the wrong word for the proprioceptive richness of sense required here!) detritus, industrial waste, mineral politics and spiced objects; queer topographies and digital 'enlandscaping', urban coding and decoding, the hunter and the hunted. Weirdness, intensity, distorted transmission, flavours of post-internet aesthetic; inhabited forms distortions of other literary dwellings. Shimmer, collaboration, lichen...

What would it mean to feel 'seasoned enough to calmly accept' the weird realism of the anthropocene? As Samantha Walton writes, 'there's nothing we can't get used to'; the shifting baselines of the normal require constant innovation in poetic form, moving between permeable cultures of the past and future to keep fresh tabs on the present. As poets, we must try to explain, as Rebecca Tamás puts it, how 'we've lost the real', 'without reverting to nostalgia' for some imaginary ecological plenitude. With Forrest Gander we are asking, 'if events rarely have discreet beginnings or endings but only layers, duration, and transitions [...] how does poetry register the complex interdependency that draws us into a dialogue with the world?' (2008). Resisting the petrifying, 'ecomimetic' (see Morton, 2010) tendencies of conventional nature poetry, anthropocene poetics dramatises the affective and material intensities of living in a fraught geologic now. Its mode is often ambience, irony, collage, ritual, queerness, symbiosis and plural acts of enframing; it confuses what we mean by 'Nature', evinces weird intimacies, explodes lyric voice across multiple times, states of consciousness and agency. 'When / am I going to learn?' asks Colin Herd, and we dwell in the break between asking and doing, and we also 'unlearn', as Nat Raha does, in a vibratory space of attunement, a 'sensorial ethics' for 'tuning the ordinary' where 'i / fabricate'.

In times of crisis, we look to art for nourishment, reassurance, reflection, a deeper understanding. Ecopoetics, as Jonathan Skinner reminds us, is fundamentally a kind of 'housemaking' (2001, p. 7). For the while, we are confined to our houses, under quarantine to protect those we love, and those we don't know, from a virus we barely understand. With these poems, we feel invited to redefine continually what it means to live in this trouble, to stay here, trust our adaptive ways of living, make a home amidst loss, confusion and 'the unprecedented'. We are with Björk as she sings, '*Utopia / It isn't elsewhere / It's here*'. The poems of *the weird folds* invite a constant turning over of this *it* where we situate ourselves in strange times of crisis, where we cocreate and orientate responsibly towards others and the more-than-human around and inside us. With Bayo Akomolafe, '[we] feel led and inspired to ask if quietude, if rest, if fugitivity isn't a space of reckoning *with the banal*, isn't a space of teasing out the sacred *from the mundane*, isn't a space of actually noticing that being at one's computer can be a time of quietude, a time of ancestral connections, that our imagination of what the sacred looks like often gets in the way of our transformation and that we can be enlisted in ways that are surprising and unexpected to slow down...' (our emphasis, Young 2020).

References

Bady, Aaron. 16 May 2016. 'Marie NDiaye's Transformations In "Ladivine"', <https://www.okayafrica.com/marie-ndiayes-transformations-in-ladivine/> [accessed 14 March 2020].

Björk. 2017. *Utopia* [CD]. One Little Independent: tplp1381cdx.

Felski, Rita. 2000. 'The Invention of Everyday Life.' *New Formations* 39: 15-31.

Gander, Forrest. 29th November 2008. 'What is Eco-Poetry', *Poetry Foundation*, <https://www.poetryfoundation.org/harriet/2008/11/what-is-eco-poetry> [accessed 25 March 2020].

Haraway, Donna. 2016. *Staying with the Trouble: Making Kin in the Chthulucene* (Durham: Duke University Press).

Morton, Timothy. 2010. *The Ecological Thought* (Cambridge: Harvard University Press).

— 2016. *Dark Ecology: For a Logic of Future Coexistence* (New York: Columbia University Press).

NDiaye, Marie. 2013. *Ladivine*, trans. by Jordan Stump (London: Maclehose Press).

Skinner, Jonathan. 2001. *ecopoetics no. 1*, <https://ecopoetics. files.wordpress.com/2008/06/eco1.pdf> [accessed 25 March 2020].

Spicer, Jack. 2008. 'Psychoanalysis: An Elegy', *Poetry Foundation* <https://www.poetryfoundation.org/poems/51396/ psychoanalysis-an-elegy> [accessed 25 March 2020].

Stewart, Kathryn. 2007. *Ordinary Affects* (Durham: Duke University Press).

Young, Ayana. 22 January 2020. 'For the Wild Podcast: Interview with Bayo Akomolafe', <https://forthewild.world/ listen/bayo-akomolafe-on-slowing-down-in-urgent-times-155> [accessed 7 March 2020].

Yusoff, Kathryn. 2018. *A Billion Black Anthropocenes or None* (Minneapolis: University of Minnesota Press).

Zylinska, Joanna. 2016. 'Photography After the Human', *Photographies*, 9.2: 167-186.

Foreword by Timothy Morton

Cool Shade Futures

I'm going with the basic scientific definition of Anthropocene—like all scientific definitions, it's just a description of data, of what is given (Latin *dare*, to give):

The Anthropocene is a layer of human-made materials in the top level of Earth's crust.

There's a lot of talk and worry about what it might mean. Scientists would be okay with calling it Jellyfish Surprise. It's not about words. It's about the fact that there's a layer of human-made stuff, dating back to about 10 000 BCE, everywhere. Everywhere. It's not about America. It's not about Europe. It's everywhere.

That doesn't mean that the causes of the Anthropocene aren't very, very significant, and very, very much to do with Europe and America, the biggest pile of Europe ever. Two gigantic "moments" stand out:

'The American century'—the 'Great Acceleration' of 1945, the massive data in Earth systems data.

The moment of colonialism in the early seventeenth century.

And humming in the background of all this, the basic origin of origins—the moment across the world, around 10 000 BCE, when humans settled in things that looked like the grain storage bins they had just invented, bins called houses. And storage bins made of groups of houses called cities. And a thing within and outside those cities called cattle: cows, women, capital ('cattle' means all three). And a thing beyond the cattle called Nature, scary, foreign, totally other. Radically different from the sisters and brothers of the so-called 'Paleolithic'—it's not Paleo, we still contain microbes and have tiny tips of pointy ears just above our earlobes, and our lungs are from fish swim bladders, and there are tiny crustaceans in our eyes. And we have cats, those aliens with alien slanty eyes that showed up unbidden to eat the rats that ate the corn in the house that Jack built. Somehow we act as if those things are totally severed from us, cut out like the daemons removed by the Catholic Church in Philip Pullman's *His Dark Materials* series.

It hurts. It hurts to pretend to be a zombie, a corpse that consists only of measurable lumps, endowed with a soul that is merely a thinking liquid trapped within said lumps like slime in a bottle.

To say that the Anthropocene names something great is like thinking that this poem celebrates imperialism:

> I met a traveller from an antique land,
> Who said—"Two vast and trunkless legs of stone
> Stand in the desert. . . . Near them, on the sand,
> Half sunk a shattered visage lies, whose frown,

And wrinkled lip, and sneer of cold command,
Tell that its sculptor well those passions read
Which yet survive, stamped on these lifeless things,
The hand that mocked them, and the heart that fed;
And on the pedestal, these words appear:
My name is Ozymandias, King of Kings;
Look on my Works, ye Mighty, and despair!
Nothing beside remains. Round the decay
Of that colossal Wreck, boundless and bare
The lone and level sands stretch far away.

(Percy Shelley)

What seems at first to be an index of human power becomes, for most of geological time, an index of human failure: failure to see around corners, while thinking that one can see everything, be omniscient and omnipotent, king of kings. Thinking that, while enslaving most of one's own species and all the others. The human versus nature binary is reproduced within the human itself by the man versus woman binary, the owner versus slave binary. One might as well yell "Look on my works, ye mighty, and despair!" while flushing the toilet, for all the pride it should induce. And underneath those lone and level sands, hundreds of other statues of hundreds of other rulers, in the geological—and therefore less obviously fluid—equivalent of a planet scale septic tank.

The Anthropocene is human civilization turned into an insult against itself.

Watching human beings doing this to themselves and to other lifeforms over and over again, once more with feeling, is like watching Mickey Mouse as the Sorcerer's Apprentice in Walt Disney's *Fantasia*, thinking that conjuring another band of marching brooms will fix the problems created by the previous lot. It is the plot of every tragedy, which is civilization's way of explaining itself to itself, version 2.0: the attempt to escape the web of fate wove it ever tighter. The side effect is the tragic sense that this is inevitable—which is why I would very much like it if ecological speech found its way out of tragedy mode. Version 1.0 was religion, also still in effect, also fatalist: we are severed from Eden, from other lifeforms, we have to do this thing to ourselves over and over again, it's the mark of our original sin. And version 3.0 is patriarchal philosophy, with its laws of noncontradiction and of the excluded middle: true and false are black and white and don't overlap, which is what every fake news meme wants you to think.

Look around you at the detritus, some of it a bit scratched but still functioning, like the broken screen of the computer on which I am typing this; other bits of it quite useless, to humans at any rate, lying under the soil, leaching into the groundwater, trunkless legs of stone lying under the lone and level sands. It's called the past. It's all you can see, all these viral bits and pieces, these shards, these phrases—a Roman coin, 'To be or not to be,' a conspiracy theory, the idea that eating meat is what makes you a real man.

Does what you call the present—the visible bit of the past that you are still handling and using—does that feel unpleasant in any way? Good. That means you are not insane and it means that the past, to use the vernacular, sucked. Ecological politics can't be a return to the past—that's fascism, when you take it to the extreme, using old tweets and old art, imposing it on everyone.

But just because appearance is everywhere—just because *the past*, which is simply what appearance really is, is everywhere—doesn't mean that appearance is everything. What a thing is, as opposed to how it appears, is everywhere invisible, withdrawn, real yet inaccessible. Even by the thing itself. If a soccer ball could speak, what it said about itself would be soccer ball autobiography, not the soccer ball soccer ball. If you kick one you get a soccer ball kick. If you measure one, you get a soccer ball measurement. If you write a poem about one you get a soccer ball poem, and since dogs can kick and robots can measure (and so on), there's nothing particularly special about human accessings of soccer balls. Like skulls, one day soccer balls will find themselves in the ground too, interpenetrated with worms like the skull of Yorick in *Hamlet*. Their use in football matches is just a brief part of their lives.

Soccer balls are hidden, even from themselves, 'withdrawn,' they have a shadow side, an opacity, a mystery that is irreducible. *Mystery* comes from the Greek *muein*, to close the lips. "Mmm" is what you say about a soccer ball when you aren't able to open your mouth. What are soccer balls? We don't know—yet...the robot doesn't exhaust their essence by measuring them and the dog doesn't exhaust them by kicking them. This intrinsic not-yet quality of a thing is what a thing is. To be blunt, *the essence of a thing is the future*.

Form or appearance is the past. Being or essence is the future. Look at one of the poems in this book. So many decisions, deliberate and not, to lineate just so, to put an internal rhyme there, to describe this using that trope. You are looking at the past. The past is infinite, meaning uncountable (not meaning going on forever). Who wrote the poem? A human being? The human's social context? The economic system around during the decade in which it was written? Stomach bacteria working on the brain? When was the poem written? Last week? In the twenty-first century? The time of humans on Earth? The Anthropocene? Where? Sheffield? Europe? The Milky Way galaxy?

All these things are true. Truths can overlap. Truths can be multiple and contradictory.

Massive scale things such as the Anthropocene force us to see how things are infinitely authored, how their pasts are infinite.

But their future, what they are, is also infinite in the sense of uncountable. Just exactly what is this poem anyway? What does it mean? When will you understand what this sentence means? How do you know how this sentence will end, elephant, black hole, parenthesis, period? And is its meaning off the edge somewhere, 'over there'? You won't find the meaning in the sentence. You won't find life in a virus. You won't find how to live in a shard of pottery or an old misogynist pattern of behavior. If you think the piece of broken statue or swastika has intrinsic meaning, you are going to cause a lot of violence.

No, what that poem is, that's an uncountable not-yet, that's the future.

Appearance is everywhere. It's like saying 'ideology is everywhere.' Quite right. Anything can be weaponized. But that doesn't mean that 'everything is ideological.' That's like saying 'everything is a lie'—'everything is a lie' must be true, so not everything is a lie so 'everything is a lie' can't be true. Ideology is everywhere, but that doesn't mean it's everything. The past is everywhere, but that doesn't mean there is no future, no possibility that things can be different.

The Anthropocene: a gigantic swath of pastness, extending all around us, back until 10 000 BCE. A past that in no way exhausts the possibility of a different future.

Poems, in this sense, are shards of the Anthropocene. They are also, as Percy Shelley observed, shadows from the future. We aren't alienated from some natural past. That's what religions, tragedies, fascisms say. We are alienated from the future. But its shadows are everywhere. You can use poems to find it, because, as I'm saying, they literally come from it. Or, more accurately, they literally are it. Poems are the future sliding against the past, in a crisscross or chiasmus that doesn't touch. Poems tremble and breathe because of that, just like everything else. They shimmer without being pushed around. You know what that means? That means things can be different. The lone and level sands may stretch far away in the burning sun of global warming, but that doesn't mean the cooling shadows of the future can't be found, everywhere you look. Everywhere you look, a portal. How to step through them, that's the trick. That's why you're reading this book.

Part One

Pratyusha

prophecy   → It's a forest fire

There is a prophecy: blue grasses flown in from
      the sunset, sweet and high, floundering for some
         other earth. I can't breathe, but it's worth it

for the shaking blue. In the dark a friend slips out
      slides like a fish down the window, scales glittering.
         The grasses are blurred at the edge of my sight,

cold afternoons rising, rising: I don't know
      what season it is anymore, I don't know if seasons
         exist anymore. What was it Gulzar said years ago:

बफ़ीर्ली सदिर् यों में / in the snowy winters —
      I haven't seen snow on these slopes for years.
         The dream is swollen with pain. A single leaf is

tired and at war. A single leaf is losing its morale.
      A single blade of grass wavers back and forth,
         sliding between times, unsure where it belongs.

It wants spring, but it's autumn. Or perhaps it's
      summer with a tinge of monsoon. The leaf tries
         to shake its insomnia and grow. Memory seeps

41

through the branches, tinting it green like an
     ache again, robbing the blue away. If only for
         a flammable minute, paused in black smoke.

Kashif Sharma-Patel

bam bam brilliance

rinse   in   out

    recoil

                 reverb

feel —   between kaffir leaves

> having a particular PH,
> 7 = neutral

    and alkaline promises

masc presents — *bam bam*
           brilliance

           seized /

          doubling visions

       detoxing   integral

   'pre - sexual'

   post - doing

multiple visions

sovereign frailties

panto   /   the news at 10

political waffle   *this week*

flashes of film

functional

working with desire / that thing on the tip of the brain keeing
    things
running, lingering

cultural history doesn't tell base   –   *femme*

social reproduction   –   that keeps going

moments with filled in gaps

hard times // pink nighties

hard to look in face of –

48

Jay G Ying

- "The sleep of reason produces monsters"

- Goya's inscription → warns that we shouldn't be governed by reason alone

death ode (XI) *dreaming*
sleep of reason → death?

did you know
this dreaming is for monsters

one sleep of reason *, made of stone*
one golem's hand slipped into the earth
I half bury like a stem from a glass
half of one inert ritual *inerte*
keeping house my fingers churned that lopsided clay and
    gulleting in the tall grass *refers to egrets*
in the white graves
those fat egrets waited by the stream for their sweet breads
    aironi

like a map each new world opens with a knife to the body and
    inside I find a sweet receipt
that paper slip
the conjured word I did not know was so untranslatable.

Prodigal *nome proprio perché è maiuscola*
what were your wonderings about

↳ prodigal = son/daughter
that leaves home then
changes their mind and
goes back

53

death ode (XII)

did you know
I lost my bearings for these ciphers

when the hysterical fugue lifted our towns swallowed
their old modes like pills
twenty-first century ghosts
made a resort of those virtual great lakes
I pricked my lip on the last artificial rose frozen by the banks

I found rest in the lantern car husks
I found life in the smouldering train carriages
red fox wisps sneering by the overturned first class
dining carts
grief struck serow herds slow and sonorous and circling

so bury me off the path
and as testimony let our bulbous sun
irradiate the last duet of green herons jousting overhead
I was unaware of those cells which multiplied within me
where's the glory inevitably killing the dead twice over.

Home
if I could get right home that would cure me

- hysterical fugue → temporary
                          dissociation /
                       loss of identity

- virtual tour of the great lakes

Sarah Cave

melograno come frutto
da mangiare il primo dell'anno?

after the end & other sibylline utterances

'a Hebrew boy bids we leave this house and go to Hades'

& yet no, we find death cradled w/ the lizard
a pomegranate halved, the end revealed
like reptile eggs, the end as we knew
this beginning we fucked up
baby's feet resemble pilgrims their endgame
is here where we are again licking toes
crushing friends like plastic
the bin tarred & feathered – our rituals
of weather burn the soft cloud
bursting berries as breasts are better than wine
bees dance for money, sorry, honey don't
she said tread on toes soft-bellies perfumed
mouths they slaughter young goats in the garden
rich w/ shrieks of ancient fragrant firs
now rafters in the meeting house
teams of dancing Shakers know more than we
about endings we see the sacred grove diminish
a sequence of slides held in a viewfinder
a poster in the lobby recalls the dead
entrails of a frog read like breath, gelatinous
like spawn we read tea leaves filtering prophesy
through teeth exhibiting the poem's ability

[handwritten annotation:] a grave? If the friends are plastic, bin must be a grave?

to comprehend finality as less than final
by calling forth rhythms; the altar,
a gash, a blue marble madness

where are they now

exeunt the pilgrims

the temple is empty
now, alone w/ the Oracle,
i fantasize about dancing
the Argentine tango w/ the pope
– his favourite. No fuss
simple shoes, silver cross,
a shepherd leading his flock.
We were made
for courting.

SOL SLICE: the science of spoken mouths

Before calling on God to save him, Jonah listens to Cetus' Song of Sheol

speaketh the seer: escapee u live w/ me now so
wuTH in n my mOUseTH owTH ooSH thou see
w/ ears the sea the sour ear of the sea corn
in my eAR the conCH is jo   NA   ha
imprisoned w/ CH eat us
an earring of them his BOdy BEEached &
blanching in equal dis stand of sun his skein a
summer blowstorm
blOW ssOMs   polaris spEAks
of colder nights & the mOOn disappEArs behind
the sea's ear we hold
& beak the sKY-tide jelly we find on SONdays
SOMweir – river run, river run – INTER state
tyre dust and heat cow n tiNG
apple blossMS w/ Eve blown like glass OW blousy bloom
SHhhh the lyre spEAks this is
winCH TH hum the thuMB muST
be Y the homOW the phone in the wastebasket
LO the LOUTH an eneMY joNAha sing
    ing in my MO w TH
complaiNT ing ChAP lain plAIn tea
God's plain tEA the sea the sOW the tEAk-up of

the sEA held to the wall of the whale-bloCK tea
NM mint this spEArmint spERMaceti listenstING
you worry the nINevENs won't like yOU

'From the belly of Sheol, I cry out'

Samantha Walton

from *bad moon*

i wake at last
to mourning
sucking pearls from irises
it was never my intention to leave you
catalytic on the shore
something like a cop over each eye
rolling parallels of the police state
a cigarette
in your palm
your chest
flowering tobacco
damp & salt-licked

*

i like oceans, sorry
have a perfect patience for minerals
the way the light is trapped in shells
comic insistence of
what we now call death
too sad to be ironic
we laugh, kiss or slip fingers into hollows
the miniature ballerina of flowers
anything to live insistently

to see what's left in best intensity
hands cupped over eyes
holding 'beauty' close as a study in
'beauty' framed by the new sincerity
the desire to give something away without
incurring a debt we can't afford

on the shore next day
we find a shoal of mackerel
their silver coats
puckered
grey &
parched
all washed up
you take a stick to
split one up inside
gross! you cry
the organ like a soup
i lay a handkerchief on top
white & knotted twice
call them an army
you say
each shrill & unnamed soldier
call them a knot
for the untying

so now, we watch the sky
take turns as the light phases
to write words on the sand
nothing is damaging
the weird scream of the starlings
gone
nothing is final
watch out for fires
they say
taking cover in the soil
watch for the streak of stars
like faces under glass

*

or rather, oil
the wild sheen of electronics
scratch of blood beneath the skin
marking lunar passage
there's nothing we can't get used to
like rocks bursting into flames
the way the eyeball ruptures
scream of gulls, song of the long dead sea
where the lawns are fire & the voice of white suburbia
is condensed to its perfect frequency

no one has time to be clever
to make considered remarks on the landscape
i must take tea, hot & dispersed
i must eat biscuit, age in cool proximity
shout out at random things like
the fog is poisoned!
the fog, curling through the lock
the caryatid press of it
thick in nose & throat
the heavy parse of industry
oil, cleaving to the gut
scent in the deepest cell

Rebecca Tamás

Whales

These are the whale dreams, coming again as they always do. Huge whale breaking over the side of the ice, too huge to make sense. I know this is the real – is it trying to tell me something? And what is that thing? Sitting in meditation class, I can't believe the feedback, 'sitting quietly for five minutes was relaxing,' 'I felt at peace.' Peace? My mind is buzzing, hornet raw, to sit with the real and confront it. In the dreams I am so desperate to see them that I feel sick, sodden with being, watching them break the skin of the water is better than any sex you've ever had. I am in a daily fight with language to explain that we've lost the real, without reverting to nostalgia. The real trying to come in over the hull of the boat. In Kolkata, it was hail like I've never seen it, large as oranges, covered in bristles, smashing through tin rooves and flattening crops, lifting a smell of citrus from the broken leaves. A woman walking a bright white horse through the seashore on Eigg, as the wind made the black sand crackle and sing. The real is not friendly, but we cannot say it is unfriendly exactly. The crest of a whale through smooth water, my body in the waves, trying to whisper out loud that I will die eventually. Feeling all of my dead forebears on me like mushy sticking leaves. The sun a big broken billboard, just read it out. The light will whack you and whack you until your tongue unfurls, relents.

Daisy Lafarge

. Albatross → mobile phone
. Here → email

* climate crisis as simultaneously
  overwhelming and distant
  phenomenon

* individual to
  its environment

a kind of alienation   *
that works in
2 directions

emails   reflection of human
(distance)   relationships through
                       insects

(handwritten annotations)
→ used to measure the significance of data

is it romantic? threshing away
∧ e) touching/feeling each other out
serious matter   predators,
                         parasites,
to emout ↑   the minuscule
     absent

p value

We'd been emailing about insects. It had begun with the inhabitants of our houseplants – aphids, fungus gnats. On the surface our concerns were purely domestic. But when asked where do they come from? it was obvious that neither of us cared about pest control. Instead we were unhealthily curious about the insect-plant relationship. Was it destructive? we wondered, or co-dependent? Our stewardship of the plants had made us spectators of their demise. There had to be gainers and losers; we craved the details shamelessly.

(handwritten annotation)
→ shift to lyric - I

I'd been writing about parasites. In the section of my ecology textbook titled SYMBIOTIC RELATIONSHIPS there were neatly demarcated subheadings; mutualism, commensalism, parasitism. I had to keep reminding myself that parasitism was a type of symbiotic relationship, not its opposite. That "symbiosis" wasn't a synonym for ecological harmony. I wondered if the people who kept using the s-word in exhibition blurbs and event descriptions knew what kinds of relationships they were endorsing.

(handwritten annotation)
symbiosis = love!

2nd shift

You'd been thinking about angler fish. For years the male of the species was believed to be a parasite, who, born with the bare minimum of sensory organs, can only mature sexually once attached to a female. The unformed male clings to the underside of his mate and injects an enzyme into her body that enables procreation. This same enzyme then dissolves the male down to his sex organ. Fertilised, the female carries around the shelled husk of the male on her body. I wondered if the female is conscious of the male's role in her conception, or does she experience herself as parthenogenic? It seemed to me that the parable of the angler fish was concerned with resplendent hybridity.

→ accusatory?

she has balls! u don't

again

She'd been looking about for an explanation. A phylogenetic tree that could neatly classify her feelings and thoughts, fears and desires. It would be a system with an index and a glossary, a list of illustrations. That way she could easily verify what kind of relationship she was in, rather than this aimless swimming through textbooks, failing to locate a phylum to anchor to her mood. Someone had suggested to her that lack was an edge-less edge, constantly remade by motive forces of desire. She thought about the incompatibility of two sponges, each one trying to soak the other up. Then she tried to think of the word for a relationship where neither organism benefits. Perhaps this was so ubiquitous that it didn't need a term? She thought about the white space between the lines in her textbook, how

/ gainers and losers,
romance and scientific interest
are combined

* Whale fall → occurs when a whale dies at
sea and the carcasses create complex localized
ecosystems → sustain organisms for decades

→ personal and planetary health

much still lurked there, waiting to emerge into terminology.
They'd been dreaming about pepper maggots and overripe
fruit. It had come up because of the zombie worms. They'd
been reading about whale fall, the resting place of a whale who
dies at sea, the slow decomposition of its body on the ocean
floor. The zombie worms mate inside the whale bones, then
eat them. Does a whale drop dead mid-swim? they wondered.
They'd read that the alternative to whale fall was washing up
on a beach. Out of water, the whale's heat-conserving blub-
ber becomes a furnace. They didn't know which was worse –
zombie worms, or boiling alive inside your own heat reserves.

→ also decadence of species.

A few evenings earlier she'd been out walking on the hill and
found a dead bee in the middle of the path. She knelt down and
picked it up by the papery wings, gently prodded a finger over
its body. Soft, surprisingly sturdy. Did the bee drop dead in the
middle of its flight? The idea of a sting drifted across her mind,
which she dismissed, because the act of stinging was surely
what had caused the bee to die. She had believed unquestion-
ingly since childhood that a bee's sting was its Achille's heel,
and conferred on the species a benignity that set them apart
from wasps, who stung with pagan abandon. But things didn't
seem so simple any more. Doubt ebbed through her fingers
and her interaction with the bee, a tentative holding which was
over and underwritten by her thoughts, which – like wasps –
weren't to be trusted.

too much oxygen → life
without air
3 levels – micro –
middle – macro

loop?

81

At home she wrote in the back of her textbook: *the mind is the body's parasite*

And she resolved to dispose responsibl y of her pesticides.

maybe you ←
cou save femininity
from male parante

- y chromazonic
- origin of species

Jane Hartshorn

→ see Tommy
   Pico for comparison
        4 dissertation

< soul , idea of transformation,
< mass   secular, spiritual
              ↓
      interplay bt < soil
                     soul

→ shift in consciousness
              ↓
     lyric speaker becomes
         the Jellyfish
→ parallelism with oil spill
      in the ocean
→ jellyfish in the intro

→ ghastly, abject < weird / everyday } improvised forensic

→ space for poetic reflection

Jellyfish

seashore, literal, literal

I touch it with a stick
push the round edge of a stone
into the pale bruise of its belly

} forensic, but also sadistic

the pop and suck of something → it has eaten something
just below the membrane → violation, penetration ? ✻
surface ripple as it adjusts its position
the lurch beneath my sole
as I stand on its gelatinous mass   baking ?   oddly
rivulets of scar tissue thickening   sensuous   → liminal space bt
as my shoulder dislocates and my abdomen   life ⟋ ⟍ death
presses its bald head into the silt
the pink daub of my mouth now
the squeeze of a lugworm
my hair a festoon of oral arms
unknotting motes of plankton
where the light percolates
the steady drizzle of excess waste
is like the clarity of absence → jellyfish's stomach
or the relief when nothing more
can be done
'how long is a piece of string'
says the surgeon
when I ask him how long it will take

✻ mimicking sexual act

fascination with jellyfish being
out of their element, they're waiting
for the tide → playing dead

87

I close my eyes and float
the vibration of metal coils
a peristalsis of sound
like the sickening feeling of the gut
as it clutches the bolus of food
but forgets what to do with it
the sound of someone clearing their throat
again and again
the pulsating bell of the jellyfish
as it pushes through water
the expansion and contraction of translucent tissue
the ripple of the digestive tract
as I travel further down the tube
held in a rhythmic wave of light and shadow
the lesions brightening like nebula
as my protons realign
and as I dissolve I think of the jellyfish
evaporating on the sand
inarticulate open-ended vessel
spilling without feeling

→ electroshock

- scientific register
  is combined with literature ○

- prophecy for poetry, ≠ stylistic
  registers

Francesca Lisette

ANCESTRAL ETIQUETTE

get up. lie down. listen in to the keen sound of rain falling,
river in your hand, fluted octave wrenching its giddy eyelid
to sell. FOR SALE. be-held. in sand dunes under a whisper of
fate, the disintegrated tropics reverberate coolly. to a bass
sound. ripe heads swing, doughy peaches among the lilac
intensities of sliced steel – brimming with carbonic emotion
the rusted engines couldn't beat out of you. curve. in prisons
of blank water, denizens murmur thunder against crumpling
walls. decisions are yet to be made, & that hurts. lines are
yet to be seared across the face & cheeks, cast hurtling into
predictive jogs: a civilizing well-used ball. falling apart. that's
what they did. split anchor & token , blood frothing & stain-
ing wood carried out to tide. in this place. the soft casting of
fingers over small ill-animated droplets, counting hunters by
their shadows. until. one day there were none. none but silent
whales, a dark magnitude thriving on a south-westerly wind.
how did you get here, i wonder, my knees at your throat. the
peculiar rhythm & hum. unobtainable. speech, something
of the Voynich. desert fingers shrugging up in bewildered
spires. will i take it. chew your forest gum & lie there like
that, all precious & unresistant, fleeting. a sensuous image in
time blared out by the stark sun. a rainbow a stitch a plunge
a throw a stone a trophy a murder a line a porpoise, a whale.
slow ache that won't stop the dam, even a blanket of cold

fire. shoot your lights, try to trace it. an unmapped country,
my body. until the rains came. & then the horizon became
a mound of sticks, heaped tinder, glue & mortar. of what
nature is a wound's relation to language? stay your hand. spill
yourself: fail to know me. plunder yet your hands hold noth-
ing but flakes of gold foil. impossible to touch. dark unsung
oyster. leave my shell to the ones who still bleed, let them
drink this liquid & fill its empty. with petrol. with grass, chalk,
emanations, piss, dreams. beyond the window a clamour: fish,
sailing over land.

*Written on the traditional lands of the Whadjuk Noongar people,
known to them as Boorloo – now called Perth, Western Australia.*

Max Parnell

Cephalopod Gambiarra

Gambiarra - the Brazilian practice of makeshifts, the art of resorting to quirky and smart improvisation in order to repair what doesn't work or to create what you need with what you have at your disposal.

I.

spinelessness
  no absence of
  mischief and craft
  a nervous system
of embodied cognition
played in limbs
and eyelids
that sample
environment for scents
carried in salt
water shallows
searching for objects
in the polychromatic shrubs
of a sponge garden
a single bottle cap
an array of shells

99

hung as marker
above a temporary → *a parallel universe*
portal *we don't have*
access to

II.

fingers darting from
two coconut shells
resting on the seabed *fondale marino*
tentacular reckoning as
hues alternate
the glint of
azure, fuschia, parakeet
coruscating in warmer waters
thin limbs tiptoe
across the sand
towards a stained → *glass house effect,*
glass house *not just glass*
hidden in *accumulated in*
algae curtains *the ocean*

marvellous in the everyday
→ *rebellion against productivity*

→ *gerund, action turnt into an object,*
poem is in action in its ~~/~~ustion,
but nothing really happens
in the poem

III.

below a fishing boat
the crab cage descending
towards octopolis → real and fantastic → contamination of the fantastic also?
jet propulsion
corporeal realignment
an indefinite shape
adapting to
mazes of iron mesh
fibre optic slenderness
whirring inside
attenuated lines of muscle
which pass through
a keyhole → perhaps connected to { glass house algae curtain
threads of neurons
clutching at chitin → main constituent of exoskeleton
as skin folds for a silent
exit, the only trace
a cluster of
broken exoskeletons → carcasses, image of death/decay
scattered across
whose wooden deck

↳ only an invitation
to continue
the poem.

→ epiphany, moment of vision

Calum Rodger

3 ecchoes for ecco

in home bay the sky
is #4265c5
and its yamaha tones
are like untelephones
the bivalves and fish
are pastoralish
in water so pure
my ecco, allure
all my sport is with you
in the ecchoing blue

full as a glass
in a convex glass
arcadian sprite
unteach and delight
to glaucous abandon
my pixeled zuhanden
thy pod and thy pond
my water'ssplashsound
all my sport is with you
in the ecchoing blue

till a fateful leap
renders depth of the deep
in water made bare
with fear and with care
so we die my dear sprite
for a bit and a byte
as thy sonar antiphon
intimates polygon
but ecco,oh, all my sport is with you
in the ecchoing blue

the marks on your head look like stars in the sky
ecco is sprite is pixel is cartridge is tide
is dolphin is cursive is form is contentment
is lowercase is being is natural is lsd
is play is be is essence is real
is illusion is innocence is vapour is digital
is moon is magic is beauty is clearing is star
is 2d is sesame is sustain is hippy is release
is being is being is being is being
is eden is cosy is intimate is sine
is haunting is real is divine is happy is ecco
vortex is feeding on the seas of our earth
vortex is polygon is texture is loadscreen is telos is
avatar is autocorrect is formal is content is
grammar is ontology is nature is ketamine is
game is mean is appearance is real is
illusion is experience is wave is analogue is
phase is trick is sublime is cleaving is rock is
3d is cheatcode is attack is punk is decay is
ego is thought is speech is discourse is
sin is cold is vast is sawtooth is
haunted is sensuous is human is trying is echo
if we breathe air why do we live beneath the waves

now as then
the most beautiful game
of the 16-bit era
is impossible

despite (or because of) the infinite
lives ecco the dolphin
this heroic dolphin
star-spelt eco-arche-agonist

who must defeat vortex
to save their pod and all of life
fails, fails utterly
in these small palms –

but i loved you ecco, years ago
when my heart was full of frosties
and i long for you this evening
amid these terrible acoustics

pretending there's a message
in the game i never finished
the promise of an ocean full
of you and other objects

ecco, if we breathe air why
do we live beneath the waves
i who is an echo of atlantis
have made these glyphs for you –

the marks on your head
look like stars in the sky

Part Two

Miranda Cichy

Winter with fallen pigeons

It is evening and the last
pigeon is scattered through the garden
like confetti, the only snow
we'll clear this year.

We find them everywhere, ~~is~~ ? why this image
little unstrung harps, blue necks
bowed in apology.

Some are a crime scene, the insides outside.
Some are unblemished, saints preserved.

My friend the artist
gathers their bones for paper.
And we go on writing, all of us,
feathers in drifts at our doors.

& antilope azruya

In the museum

The piece that bothers me most
is the bluebuck skull, tucked in a corner
under the soft blue light of evening.
It's not the grimace, nor the monstrous horns
giving their keratin two-fingers, or even how
bluebucks were thriving in the glacial age
and humans wiped them out by 1800.
No, it's that the skull stays bare,
fixed in rictus, sockets eyeless,
won't sprout a body, won't unbuckle
wobbly femurs and stand, pace around
the parquet, tell me how the bluebuck
ran or suckled young, tail swinging.

It is small comfort to think upon
the world ruled by bluebucks,
where my skull is gaping on a rock,
peeled like an orange, and its visitors
imagine how I moved or ate or died.
Where the bluebuck child cocks her muzzle,
renders me four-legged, furred,
her mind's eye building up our pack
which gallops over concrete fields
with useless, hornless heads.

Her forbears scuff their hooves
against the pavement, skulls down.
They will gore us into history, one by one.

Albatross

[handwritten: Romanticism]

the last time that I saw you I'd seen photographs of
    albatrosses
with their stomachs full of lighters their bloated stomachs
    open
                           [handwritten: activity in Dark]
on a galaxy of colour bottle tops combs fishing lines *[handwritten: wire]*
the sky was boiled water and the room had blue curtains
your hair was feather light and flying I held your wrist trying
to remember everything they had given you a child's cup
a beaker with two handles your hands shook as you raised it
to suck the warm sweet tea you didn't understand my phone
could take your picture I left it in my bag trying
to remember everything not to think of albatrosses
those dead white birds like paintings stomachs full
of buttons tampons biros toothpaste lids ping poll balls
your cup placed on the tray before the nurse brought in
a plate of mash and gravy your finger lifting pointing
the last time that I saw you pointing at your plastic cup
saying isn't this the most marvellous thing?

*[handwritten: * boundaries bt < inside ? blurred / outside]*

[handwritten: Albatross -> connected to human body]

118

eschatology → how do we
articulate
the end of days

* parallel between { bag
albatross,

the kind of things you would
have in your bag

· Lyric feeling, desire to house
memory

· These objects do not deteriorate

· Human memory, memory of phones

· Marvellous → points to a loss of
memory, cup becomes
a marvel

Alice Tarbuck

Musee de la chasse et la nature

In the   forest   highest days of
summer   august of that year

Before the   first high hedges   kingdom
fell   drought   particularly set in

We see the   virile man   [his
portrait here]   nature's emperor

Bestride the   times   the burnished
saddle   the thrilling scene

Blackbird and lark are   silent
        absent   silenced

The players gather for the chasse, and so it can begin.

In the forest
friezes fix forms, plaster moulding
how heavy the roses, how still all the leaves, how
bristling the briar transfixing itself,
horses scrolling over green ground that heaves
wet secrets, leaf litter, the damp smell of houses
where ruin has set.

Beside the glass case of feathers which is
silent   cooing   taking flight
a bristle of fur, the stag
steps across the clearing glade   drawing
room,
beneath a tapestry of himself, lovingly stitched
in which they imagine him,
nothing but meat.
Complete, he blank-eyes the soft hangings.
Someone has made a copy of him,
undraped his skin,
blown him in glass, all movement carbonised,
vitreous warped, enchants the eye which pans,
wolf-whistles the length of him.

Before the camera pulls away, Beritola suckles
fawns, falls
in love with a dry doe, unweakens all her
woman's skin, grows hide
demonstrates that strength need not attend with
dogs or antler's push,
milk-tied, tree-tied, herbs and cold water: love
that is sweet amid the bitter
she hangs up her city-dress on a glass stag's
antlers.

Everyone who enters the forest
is an oak tree   a suicide   a citizen
scientist
everyone who enters is enveloped by the soft
mouth
of a dog,
is touched by the faery king's horse
as he slips past, his hunt
the opposite of mercy
and all his stock-taking of the taken things
unfathomably high.

The faery-king's retinue pools out like a cape, the
admission charge:
gilded crossbows, shadow, a dance between the
trees
that takes our naked bodies, lithe and pleased,
stretches them out beside the guns.
And he is   glittering   threatening
          divesting
his loveliness, and he is writhing with, we must
assume,
pleasure in the forest's armoured room
and wants us to take aim.

He would let us in, all wickedness, to do what
harm we may,
because the forest is terror.
His meticulous fingers over ours whilst he sings
trigger songs, loves guns the way that hunters do:
bringers of glory, all pain
etched, engraved away, made fine with leather,
sheathed in velvet, tipped with gold and steel that
bears stag-pictures, pictures of whatever
triumphant thing
has been brought low. The steel bears images of
us, we know.

In the dining room   the boudoir
        the sacred glade
six courtesans have been employed
to list dead birds for us, all narrow shouldered, all
snarling or all innocent.
The falcons roost there, sawdust stiff, the
courtesans pluck feathered tails
to trim their hats, to touch each others' chins. In
silhouette
a feast of songbirds open up their throats.

In the forest   the railway terminal
      the formal gardens

Ekphrasis pants the hunt, the tear, the twitching
dream.
Ekphrasis at the soft mouth, throws the ball
beyond
the king's dog-chamber, lets it roll
back to the wide oil paintings.
You cannot smell the game stench, reach to peel
the pheasant whilst his flesh
is warm, take his
skin off tenderly like the king's robes, reverent,
the way I have in the kitchen. That costs extra,
and is not
included with the audio guide.

II In the gallery of mounted heads

Inspectable, the necks protrude, and you put your
hand against them. You feel the stuffing, where
formerly the larynx lived, you close your eyes
and imagine the taut fear caused by a human hand
around the neck, the *in in in* of breath. You put
your mouth to them when the attendants are on
their break, and you can think about blood, and
press your lips against little splits of their DNA,
go home throat-lined like dead stag's neck,
choking on it
but you can't do anything useful except bristle
kiss, and that's the sort of worship
gets you kicked out
for being a writhing sentimentalist.

I am not sure how many extinct things you can
look at before you become one or
before you are sick, and I wonder if there is a lot
of distinction between types of evacuation, bodily
and planetary.
I want to sit down on the velvet chaise and have a
head between my thighs whilst I talk about the
best of my departed things.
The faery-king keeps asking

if I'll eat, and this encountering is hungry work.
He says
I can change all my iron for gold but I'm telling
him my pocket knife
is more than I'll surrender. Let me see your horse,
I say.
a mare of bone and shadow,
built from ivy leaves and gilded flakes of mica.
The guide asks me not to sit on the furniture. It is
notedly delicate.
The faery-king speaks in the forest through the
skulls of animals
that look like our own. He talks through the
gleam of the guns.
He sits at night on a chair made of antlers, bent
low to the ground,
and his courtiers are all the stuffed creatures
who roar with laughter at his jokes
and ably lose at cards
because they know a threat even when it is
dressed
in soft silks and playing petanque across the
museum floor.
Everyone's gun is always with them, carried
by a valet, who stalks, pleasantly unremarkable,
awaits

some analysis of himself as anti-pastoral,
as an economic marker, as an incursion of rural
selfhood
across the scene. The museum is full of the dead,
the forest is full of the sun, silts the trees with
gold on all their brown
and the faery-king sinks down in the saddle of his
most

expensive horse, whose back is lean, whose
flanks
are testaments of breeding. Someone has flattened
out owls
across the ceiling, to make decoration somewhere
between handstroked paint
and screaming, as if the stars were pulled apart
and given beaks and eyes.
Don't worry, says the guide, they are all already
dead. As if you had thought... – and so you spend
the rest of your time
wandering from case to case
your fingerprints a dirty mark on polished glass
aware that all these things were once
alert   desired   alive
and the deer goes back to meet, and the almost-
forest writhes.

fred spoliar

talk / show / ghost

full employment, a talk show, an eclogue, a Castle, central Late Capitalism

Welcome to [███████████████] – Where Truth Operates
A crazy white horse --------------reared from our charmed moat
Or "couch" --
-----------& powers the town. (Not moot, moat!)
(Not the lyric truth, the truth!)
To enter the Castle, please select from the following options:
{~~Host, Guest 1, Guest 2, Guest n+1~~, the horse}
To play as the horse:

▶   ctrl+h
▶   find: words ["the windows to the X"] (see: factor)
▶   replace: dumb sounds (see: great (noisefull) Silence)

This can signify

1. a choke 2. a sort of transcendental lack of (boo) the Subject
in the face of script-assured {Guest 1}s.
Spare me, [Cumberbatch],
your craft and method,
that gas. Ask me about the horse
That never happened. Ask o (nought) of me. What *tapestry*?
Birds of Paradise ~~vanishing~~ on main

by the 3rd degree I sat down and   couldn't tell you
what tapestry --------- Robotniks couchant
- o exhausted squinting golf course o argent –
load up ~~your muskets, noble friends~~
the ~~goodly~~ wasteland ~~to maintain~~

                             ►

Something is rotten in this Magic Eye.
        Nature sounds
          Pregnant with
the drawbridge uprising
        We begin tearing   up
whenever entering the streets   We fail   to solidify
our loss   which keeps me here
(see: the machine)   interviewed by the ghost   like a boss
As for {Guest 2}, I am the luckiest of {blue / ~~pink~~}
        I'd like to thank my
        castle syntax
        dancing to S Club in the whiteness.
        Not mortgage, kitchen. Not whiteness:
        poetry!
        […]
Who takes out the bin bins?
who made the sky / gullsore
with weeping

demolished / the ancient dwellings / of birds

✿♥✿ B E A U T I F U L ✿♥✿

correspondences
between dumb sounds made / now for the sky :
{Host} burns them
    and leaves
        the system flooded
with requests
    that redirect to a

Page not found

and doesnt {Guest n+1} just cry at the sheer fucking pathos
of it all

Where..is the former Bird?
What...was its coloured light?
Who...its afterlives of soft geometry
        , when inauthentic plumage leaves
        me unwaged and hound-dog on the.......

                                            "strip"

and after all
Did I {Guest n+1} fail – loving you {The Castle} – to improve
                        from old french to   profit
                from the "immortal soul" did I evolve
business models that will support a data-driven ecosystem

?   {yes NAND no}   intensifying water stress,
                                      dumb sounds
                                      [...]
Lie down here on this red carpet,
[Simon Armitage].
Read this
meme on Graceful Decay,
                                      self - effervesce to matter!
say "[Graham]... play me... a funeral march... on kazoo...
                                      now say "alas... I die..."

Iain Morrison

written-in elegy a Midlothian cemetery and churchyard

Prelude
Here in Midlothian where I think I'm stood
I've ta'en the bus to revisit sic a place as lately I came
with friends who divvied each their histories and clues
to these lowlands' map of literary fame

where William Drummond, Ben Jonson sought at
    Hawthornden,
De Quincey took refuge, and later his pals the Wordsworths
    and Hogg
all visited Scott, who was revving his writing career in situ.
A wonder that the vale's regard is dogged

by reputation as a second cousin,
post-industrial, lacking Edinburgh's cultural heft and plenty.
At any rate, dear Williams, Capildeo, Waters,
our summer's jaunt laid charms enough to tempt me

back, bound now in a more reflective mood
alone, in winter, later in the day, and lower in spirits
as it falls dark. I hold but one pre-charted aim:
o'erlooking the pub and the river's scenic merits

to climb the hill so high as where are splayed
the spokes of three successive burial places in a wheel,
there to profound my heart's investment in this place
if aught, dowsing in all the local feels.

Elegy
Not borne out here that bloods were never stirred
nor shed for nations' fame, nor likely ever was borne true,
the rudeness of the familiar Tory poet's lay made plain
where silver birch shade high-flown verse and the view's

pulled short by their lines charcoaled against the sky's
high border. On the opposing bank read, wrapped into Britain
      how
an exiled Pole as officer allied his fight, leaves honour
inscribed to the sister lost at Birkenau.

Fond solar lights by graves now glimmer on,
and artificial Christmas trees stake watch o'er what it means
to be enlandscaped now, your country, soldier, spent.
The burial ground creaks back, shuttering its beams

while I cross down to the ancient part, an enclosed
old churchyard. As if pre-fixed in ordinate time, an owl hoots
prolongedly. In a standing aisle wall's a hole
for doves, or bats, or what the evening suits

144

to ease out from the chartered space behind.
I'll meet no correlate eyes, in trust to this portioned ground
        alone
at the chilly, darkling time I call, when deterrent lighting
paid by the council safens adjoining homes.

This acreage maps discomfort out for me,
a resister of solitary states, yet frequent forgetful and
        sub-purpose spectre
I perch beneath one ruined wall on another, lower
more ruinous still, though it preserves its vector

in newer cement where iron railings were;
I feel their melted stubs run under my sitting, where they've
        been stripped
down to the base, taken away then recast for munitions,
the old war present again, rubble and script.

What of the affects of queer, pressed here in this boneyard?
For have you not visited such to sensual ends, worked out in
        seclusion,
the historic twinkling of smokers in night-time recesses, our
        lust
where it had been elsewhere snuffed, unsheathing discretion

(least otherwise snuffed, as far as the record that's passed)?
I rose here thinking of boys, hot and alive from a bus
    encounter
and shot with the fear I gave to myself when, in shorts and
    muddy
boys boarded my bus. As quick, I breathless was bounded

out of the new exit door that's been introed, the bus layout
changed, so now no face to come face to, or saying goodbye
    to the driver.
Younger than I could want, I'm indited to know if their hearts,
their rooting loins have been taught disgust, trust either

or violence to pitch up against my physical warmth,
the which could change. Unsettled now, before I can end,
    hear the reason
I came to these graves whose proxy accounts are a match
    quite close
enough for feeding into my kinship notion:

the winds that scuff the verdure topping the hollow
weather a stone that holds my name – in age its letters
    endure,
and I double-checked the font for a usual lain confusion –
named as his spouse, a male name I keep secure

and while I don't state it, attempting to serve honest doubt,
it dares me, flouts ambiguity – O witness me caught in stretch
    to claim it! –
willing that someone, some two, had lovered over the force
I transpose backwards, so really it's me in my name that

prevails, looks forward now, re-setting mid-Lothian
to fit, in a place I'd thought not mine, had been in fact
    encouraged
to think my way out of by bootstraps, and so I went and so
have kept myself, to return estranged and aged.

Sodium casts its distant, ambering light
not by itself of a brightness to show what in faith I'm
    scribbling yet,
though it makes yon clinging leaf a dancing shadow thrown
on a gable at six as dark as it ever will get.

Scott's narrator's haunt in his hours of leisure
I'll leave behind, like Old Mortality, strengthened by
    numinous elders,
these sleeved together in tomb since seventeen-something-
    or-other.
Gathering possessions I ready to helter-skelter

off on my temping route downhill. I check
the bus app, trying to be careful for mud along
    th'unpavemented wynd
and cars not visible save by their rapture of climbing lights
blindingly white in front, dulled red behind.

Epitaph
Chaturbate sweet in an easy connecting present
metal lantern flying in dangerous sky. An alarm slips on
from nearby gardens where snowmen flicker from left to
    right
and a Père Nöel's legs cycle between positions.

Dangled glisters cascade, are cracked on the river,
cross the locals' cockades and I am beyond the poem now,
not to appeal as a man who appeared one e'en like a phantom
among them unspeaking, the less to concern myself how.

Gloria Dawson

from overcruising (field notes)

i)

almost immediately I put my shame on
it is an afternoon morning itself I feel like
shame on, not a colour, but like the fasting away from touch
initial and a cold burn, whylike

it is sunny and I am shamed of how the sun has
burned the clouds clear, a spring
outlook to summer; if I stretch through
out to a turning burn that waters it,

twists itself into pewter, makes itself
concrete and adder, how does the colour
of a country make itself known
in body's sorrowspasms. this is not a portrait

of the next decade; shame on you
for wanting it to be, death-life, not
the swarm of morality that stings from holy papers, more
like the white roses moving fast through one day's

lickable armpit. the only orientation
I have for this is gay and it's not mine, I wasn't
born inside this rose's miracle and I'm only finding out
today by stinking bins that no-one's born from the solar anus.

ii)

say it tastes like the orange rind,
burnt, because we cannot give it any more
shame. common orchids don't cruise, they

root and loiter under ash, in bracken,
orchards, entwined in sorrel, commoner
than sucked dicks or success.

as a subject described as
something about which I know less than
nothing but the sun don't care, finds

exasperating, mutters *fucksake* as he lands
on another sleepless head. *on your bike?*
he asked and I was like *no, for sex.*

you can't say *poisoned with loneliness.*
doesn't sound. that's the grass
doing its wee camp holler and that's
what nothing fabricates. in order

for ART to take place, there have to be parks,
scummy and going nowhere circular, from which time

has wrested a bush and you've made it
by your doings, a palace. much rather sleep

attached to this completion than in
what are obviously other people's beds. Borage,
begonias, errant tomatoes and yes,
roses grow up past I can't imagine,

tendrils. and a heart that one, heart that
one that beats it, and no longer phrasal
hands and face and tongue and teeth and hands
with nothing under their upbraided soil

iv)

run round downed drum, run under round soil numbered,
particles of what is was, old round shit-demon, soil
breathe in case refusal's next, refuse dump yourself
for a new lover, be on a habit of fresh green, un–
cankered heart, by-passed spleen and colour theory

right down among ring-rounded mushrooms, I learnt
to breathe. at the summit, gunturret of thistles
discharges light. lights on grass and paths and bricks
old clusters with a texture august. old man's beard,
pectorals, sonnets and grasping pivots to get here,

so many seams. mycelium for knitbone ends, she;
Someone could find this but nobody is looking for me.

v)

mushroom inover fort, beech-banked in orange hear
this sight every wet pelt through the motorway sparge
and slitting every soak and gleam. hedgehogs under
white spume sitting like a batting battered hold, feel
I a very special path in all this mud. soft turkey tąil, breath
of yesterday till mushy, soft like you wouldn't breathe it.

path is liquid fingered tinder trudge I break it, breath
coming up parasympathetic avenues and making all
the sycamore look clean. anomie oak-shaped, bruising
patterns on my seams lean in under sovereignty, bullets
run the rhizome, and come, and get down, the ringroad
bronzing foundational light, pecker, vanished, green

dark plowed expression, lichen it to flabber kiss.
Someone could find me but nobody is looking for this.

Vahni Capildeo

Nocturne #4

You did not say it to me
but it spoke to me.   Traveller,
the green bottle is for the day,
the purple for night; don't you
ever sleep?

You did not say it to me
but it spoke to me.   Painter,
was this your waterfall? You gave
no label to a place we sense
quietly.

Naked people were bathing there
one time; Venezuelan voices
trickled down another time,
refreshed, for once at ease from
migrancy.

Painter, if this waterfall
high in the hills has not been yours,
make it so. Trees block valley views;
companioning minds turn inwards,
seeing you.

*You did not say it to me
but it spoke to me.*

, probs refers to dancing

Nocturne #5

Your number comes up as Unknown.
Blue cat under a car at noon.
Your number comes up on red shoes.
Pas de deux with Señor Unknown
spins you to the brink of blue roads,
red lantana in profusion;
to open and sheltered waters.

maybe use of foreign languages = unknown? or are they taking the piss?

You're sure you knew Señor Unknown
as if since the day you were born
till the day he'd pull you aside,
a dance card, a lottery ticket,
a cuneiform bill of lading
with your number on it in his hand.
A kicked jack on the table
for your game of All Ones. Instead,
sometimes he's pulling you closer,
sometimes wandering on ahead.
Sometimes he gives up the tango.
Chants you into his capoeira.
Shows you a Morpho Eugenia
butterfly, makes you think turquoise
while putting pure dark and bitter
criollo cocoa on your tongue.
As if Señor Unknown wants you

to live, preciosa, though he's
no more or less than the open clefs
carved into a violin's curve.
He gestures. You think it's a wave.
Mistake him as beckoning you.
This is a nocturne. Unbecome
the book, Reader. It's way too late.
Unknown – *waves up to two metres*
in open areas – your number
comes up – *but less than one metre* –
Precisó – *in sheltered areas* –
He wants you to live till you're dead.

Nocturne #6

Night, I'm not going to say
you aren't there. You hurt my eyes
with promises of rest; stretch
weighted blankets on warmed beds
under which the hills can crawl
starring out their masts, mansions,
scars and forests. You press hills
into your dark like a brush
wetting paper with colour.
You are high up and fluid.
Night, I'm going to hold on
to you, today, in daytime
in your absence, in your sharp
absence. In bright fluorescence
I hold to you, surrounded
by fluid darkness, indoors
and out, in scathing sunlight
darkness nonetheless sheathes me
as if I lie down on air,
high up. I have not been schooled
to see like a scientist;
therefore I know your contours
without having to touch you –
and I know you're not there, not

in that way. I am. Body
of exhaustion, frequenting
shops where natural tears are sold
by formula, with droppers;
eyes dried by overwatching,
overweeping – I am not
like that, Night. I expected
to break on you. Holding on.
The time for warning is done,
Night, now is the time for joy.

Sascha Akhtar

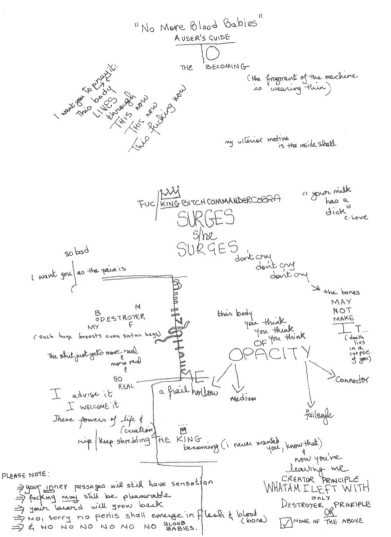

"No More Blood Babies"
A USER'S GUIDE

THE   BECOMING

(the fragment of the machine is wearing thin)

I want you to graph it.
This body
LIVES
through
THIS now
This now
This fucking now

my ulterior motive is the inside shall

FUC|KING BITCH COMMANDER COBRA
SURGES
s/he
SURGES

"your milk has a dick" c. love

so bad
I want you | as the pain is

don't cry
don't cry
don't cry

the bones
MAY
NOT
MAKE
IT...
(death lies in a corpse of you)

B   M
O DESTROYER
MY   F
(such huge breasts even satan begs)

The shit just gets more real &
more real &
SO REAL

this body
you think
you think
OF you think

OPACITY

Connector

I advise it
I WELCOME it
These powers of life & (creation)
rip | keep shredding THE KING becoming (i never wanted you, know that)

ME
a frail hollow
Medium

failsafe

&
now you're leaving me
CREATOR PRINCIPLE
WHAT AM I LEFT WITH
ONLY DESTROYER PRINCIPLE OR
[✓] NONE OF THE ABOVE

PLEASE NOTE:
→ your inner passages will still have sensation
→ fucking may still be pleasurable
→ your beard will grow back
→ No, sorry no penis shall emerge in flesh & blood (bone)
→ & NO NO NO NO NO NO BLOOD BABIES.

i want you so bad
like every now
has roses.

i want you so bad when did night fall?

i want you so bad
like pain has teeth.

i want you so bad, your
rabid sauce.

i want you so bad; the infinity
becomes you

i want you so bad
lemons. Bad, lemon.

i want you so bad
visible interrupted
shadows

I
WANT
YOU
SO BAD
VOMIT
VOMIT
VOMIT

i want you so bad
in the magical quarters

#iwantyousobad

lmao

i want you so bad, you
are integral to my argument

i want you so bad
lemon. Naughty, lemon.

pain
is
i want you so bad
when
angels
fly
in
HELL
(buttons).

i want you so bad
it is developing sharp edges
& fabricating rainbows

i want you so bad
braid me
into your
claws.

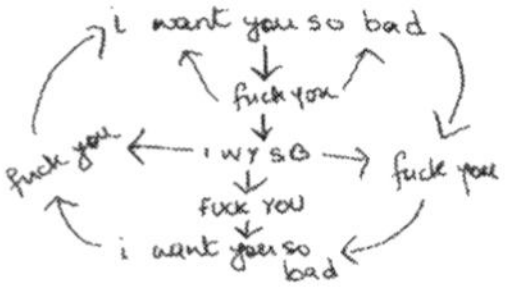

i want you so bad
fuck you
fuck you
IWYSB
fuck you
FUCK YOU
i want you so bad

i want you so bad:
join the main.

i want you so, bad
boy

i want you so bad
every season becomes

i want you so bad
hardcore smarties.

i want you so bad
it's an obvious difference
in nuance
& grind
how does water fall
upwards
& then some

i want you worse than so bad
(he knows. she knows.
they know)

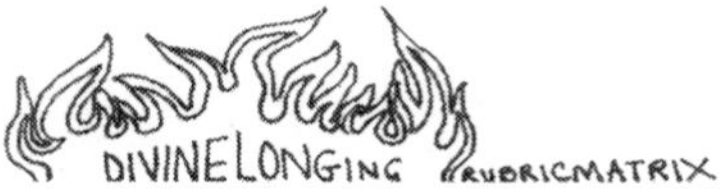

DIVINELONGING
RUBRICMATRIX

Fred Carter

habits of order (not yet second nature)

how far away, how irretrievably lost were the beautiful, free, tender-green fields of romania!
:rosa luxemburg, 'letter to sophie liebknecht,' (breslau, 1917)

by then we knew that weather was a mood and had
a history, it observed forms of intimate and martial law
entirely mute. dispatches that exceed each factured skin.

—and still,

walking the length of the denuded palácio there was
just so little furniture that the general strike felt ever
increasingly inevitable & intangible to the groceries.

—yes,

breaking into the abandoned grammar might equip us with
a sketch of shelter finally to sleep but can't alleviate the over
arch of crisis even slightly. only haunts it; saves what's let.

when we arrived at the seat of primacy, we found that the conditions
for entry shifted ceaselessly over a bucolic valley, verged with
pejorative contracts and such light under the clouds we thought,

—and

—then,

that my houseplants each resented the neighbour's airbnb as well
but even so were still complicit in their viscid shades of green. their
tendencies to yearn. their need to give and take from states of nurture.

unfreedom and distraction pattern every day, despite all.
seceding from the surface of this institution, write me.

take up arms of cloudberries when it's the season. open
letters, open wounds. sounds have gravelled under boots.

Katy Lewis Hood and
Therese Keogh

Besides cramped currents, see sores in the
rust by rope and rope and lost its
        held its bearings
            "When any public work,
              of an extensive nature
A heave and buckle, and a switching of
positions
Remember leaching goes both ways
Reeling cotton, a spin and a frame and a
sadiron cast from the smelt
 "is projected, a clear and impartial discussion
Burnt skin, fine cuts. Silt settles in and
spreads out
Sludge heaping at the edges grasps unblocked
memory of swamping
Mired desire repeats itself
            "as it affects individual property
The water sleights patinated into hand
        a skillful deception and a
        guided mirage
A grazed surface, a resurface, a piled surface
          "cannot be uninteresting
The water will have milled around the edges
of tender
   "The ductile streams obey the guiding hand
Woven steps of worn out legs

"is the art of holding and caring even while being ripped into, at the same time as being held" needs an action and an instrument but also the flesh of a thing to cut into, a grammatical and material object

a shallow lift, a callused want
Subsides, the sediments' upheft to the top
Height defined by thin boards
on hinges and weights
Released, fallen, churned
Under, the hum of gelidity
prickled skin
mumbled diversions
Dredged legs cut into running slabbed lengths
toll-taken, exaction, expent
"How much are you bearing?"
A slick reply mirrored a measured response
A stuck rimple—ored, dammed—
uneases the residue
Before slipping and dropping, and lying face up
a sloughing
The water rushed the colour of metal it carried
once and more along
It gathered grit and breathed out
not lightly
not without effort
but a raspy exhale and a dead fish
the hollow bag of waters
contracts

infrastructural forgetting: currents in canals—cuts, open wounds—levels, blocked from flowing, stopped from participating in the production of a present...will (not) heal and disappear

Strings of wells lean into chalky terraces
                    levelled vertically
                    leaking horizontally
Feet first, lips first
With each cough the damp carries
Bubbles gather in the rock's weft,
burbled ear canal
                    suspend
Chimeric exhale; coats for hushed walls,
clumped veins, small cavities
Openings fill up, clogging and bursting
and flooding
The basin as source for your harder waters
                    one lining scaling another
An enduring resolve
Softened grounds, stagnant locks:
                    exposure marks and
                    lime cordial
          "And social plenty circles round the land
Over grid to sit, the water blackens where the
works were blooming
Oxygenated heat. Orange-yellow hot
                    blue-green suffocate
Fingertips subbed for the skin of a pig
                    or a goat
                    or a cow

work locks meaning produced through movement; stopped production stuck material back wounded sense in how or by also, as a kind of through, but then not that, but more like a while ago, so much as that if not this

185

Streaming subcutaneous, undercurrent hides
colloid intimacy between
The water feeds from the matter it alters
Kneeling in mud, on bricks, reposed, and
repeated
Waters laminate and fuse, forging a fold then
pointedly asking
                    "which direction from here?"
The water lets in the faucet, pressure of
bodies kept aboveground

The well gathers the past, and its waters produce actions in the present. Past produces an open present... time is divided into past and non-past

I walked, I walk, I will walk... there's no walk in the future

montenegro fisher

treelogy
by montenegrofisher

polygraph
listens to the leaves
decolonisation
of the ear
species to spices
roots to sky
feeding the borders
defining the wasps
books to banyan
banyan to books
sandalwood or rubber
elastic band tension
roam to immediacy
cows milk to curd
enlightenment to enrichment
nutmeg revolution
pepper-powered-words
mustard seed

everlasting scent
grows necessity
government's own nature
parasitic reciprocity
Shiva dissolves form
lovers hidden in bark
saffron to earth
spiral incision
drip, drop
dribbling tyres
polyamide insanity
screening pandemic
isolation
as the crow flies
in crow-less fields
crowd-less ravens squark
limping through super-symmetry
pressure cookers
dawn chorus
sunrise

holy substances
soaps and sticks
intravenous organisations
untouchable verbs
tongue faints from lips
inner sanctum
munching termite
formless creation
dematerialised mind
mist
must-miss
mass-control
misleading instructions
moss or mouse narratives
piercing volumes
reach the gods
among the tamarind
reptile to fruit
becoming banana flower
chewed by a flying fox
genital irrigation
portable
karma

Nat Raha

after Nina Simone & Kathryn Yusoff

gorse tongue , clarity holds sky about
    yur rotations to halt / thoughtforms
                      to containment
              flaming golden high /
        orde/rings from a world once new
, the grasp becoming ownership
              , land
                    becoming territory
                    becoming soil
                    becoming igneous
                    becoming resource
                    becoming arable
                    becoming pasture

„ reading each field by fertility
each body by species, capital & surplus
values *forced to seed monofutures,, rede/finition*
of crops against indigenous & black bodies
extract myriads from spines—

        vio/lent universal, its
      mastery is the mythos that names you
      && which worlds ground in end/eavour
      , pursuit of glitz & profit a wake *all*
      on that day / structure disavowed
      blood & dirt d/ripping every pore
      smoke & horror becoming yur spec
      -ies, a lan/gouge & grammar for extinctions

day is the d/ream in
which so much relation
is severed, the city assem/bled, re
flections met illuminate, en
                -titled, natural intact
                sediment lines & di/visions,, *& i run*
                                to the river, it was boilin'
                        residing deep / phantasmic
                wildness eclipse ways of world & revolt
                & i run to the sea / it was
                boilin' to chart & map foundational
                , re/plant

  -ed arrays pave, speaking in/acti-
    ons reading each city by heat
            map, *what's*
        the matter with you
                    , rock ; architecting only future [of] you[r] own
                    ,, its effacious, genocidal subject
                                    wished to touch
the glut of human / the mine & carceral
                            means of adornment to all you

        what you wish to retain & cold,
    clench the sky to save from caving
            , freezing ≠ own sheaf ice ,
        knowledge drips your beak

198

for a sensorial ethics, unlearn
each assonance tuning the ordinary
                              daydrift i
     fabricate, known in ancestral vibrat-
               ions life giving to flesh, rise
attentive felines to who owns, add/ict
          -ing sonic & heat, out of
spines curl gradual like the year's length
winter leaves its pressure / a
          universe ringing, intoning
                         an end to crown &
               titles installed on stolen land
          aspiration to / particular & NOx down

Mike Saunders

In memory of low frequencies

The combination of a field
and a beach is a desert, pure
and simple. Close down ill-
feeling and we'll live

quietly. My heroes are planting
hazel trees between uneven
rows letting the weeds
grow up over

dry furrows. They're breeding old
strains of wheat with older strains, and it's
good but the culture is so small it
breaks my heart. I said nature

should be an emotion but now
I think it should be an action, just
as strikes are actions and happenings
are actions, just as confronting cyclical

thought is an action, just as driving
past mirrored & silent water
is an action. A golden lifeless
spiral, a parody of melancholia, a

performative aspect of inertia expanded
into a non-euclidian and vaguely
threatening wide open empty sky. There's
no air but the wind

still blows. A comfortable terror. The ragged
edges of a learned behaviour becoming
conscious. Continue to fail a life of purity, of
satedness, of absolute

equality of moderation in
all things. My interaction with fields
has become a desire for air braided
with a desire for all

the complications entangled within
the air. A burning archive, but no notion
of anything on fire. A small ringing
note catalysed by

a chill breeze. A thin song of
absorption in a collective
moment of malevolent gathering: some things
are not worth describing. Nostalgia

is a curse but nostalgia for sunlight
and heat is something else. Is it true
that a deliquescent unravelling
can predict a total effect? The airborne

can only exist at
dusk or in darkness. In my draft
of the poem I have a note
to write a section for my friends. Despite

what I've said about moss
it doesn't matter where the sun lies
in the sky, it just matters that the measurement
was co-opted from an attempted

reckoning of earthly and blinding friction
for something as capricious
and flat as capital surveillance. A specificity
of unquestioning vapour ready

to live a secret life of weakness wrapped in
the projection of a perfect being. Anyway
I'm surprised it took me
this long, honestly. I listened

to an engineer outline the possibilities
of colonising Mars - they said at best
it would be like living in an airport
and at worst it would be like

living in an airplane. If you whisper sweetly
enough sound forgives the mistake
of its own presence. True feeling
will follow. Sure the sun

pulls the moon, but the moon pulls us
and we like it. We like it that way.

Part Three

Jane Goldman

.

in this space

i-i too am likely
at this time it's three a.m. hissy purrs on my hip
she

perches coories in
at my elbow's crook purrs harder watches my
fingers type for

fuck's sake i-i am no robinson crusoe (all how
like a king i-i dined too all

alone attended by my servants) yes haecceity
hissy is with me

she co-shapes this poem
ici hissy
ici moi

bitter lemons for the dead beavers

surely one waxes to a beaver moon
there can be no waning for a poet
beaver who's out for a roasting first
prime your language traps with scent
bait of some poet already trapped wait
for some fresh heedless poet to come
by at perigee (at their fullest
and nearest in orbit—this takes fine
judgment to know a poet at their
fullest and closest in orbit) they sniff
castor bait then walk in push trigger
release dog snap voilà for a roasting never
to be forgot what could fresh headless
roast poet smell like when gently in your
gilded lycra you tug the steaming lyric
(all wordy in its word caul) place it sparkling
at the poet's breast all skin to skin i-i know
you would perform this your glitzy
midwifery
so tenderly
for any poet
yes even
and
and

and
and
and
and
and
and
and
just kidding

i-i wore my friend sharon's
granny's nineteen forties beaver
fur coat with army surplus boots
and mothed black braided barathea
dinner trews and salvaged ballantynes
woollens also mothed and diamanté clips
only a little tarnished in which to
embrace the base on greenham
common it was nineteen eighty-two
i-i was with ca it was winter we
had no money our flat-mates raised
our bus fares packed us food
wanting to end war and stuff we
baited the barbed-wire fence with
poems and pictures and ribbons
and a silk dressing-gown i-i lit
a candle and we slugged martini

in sorry sad thanks to the long dead
beavers with no choice but to keep peace
warm while we sang in semi similes she
is like a mountain breaking metaphors old
and strong she goes on and on and
on you can't kill the spirit reworking
words by naomi littlebear molena
i-i kiss her name i-i kiss her words
naomi littlebear molena

[send all your vintage thrifted fur
to PETA People for the Ethical
Treatment of Animals for use
in educational displays and anti-fur
"fashion shows" and to provide
 bedding for needy animals
 it may be too late to save
 the life of the animals who
 died to make the coat
 but PETA can put it to good use
 to help save the lives of countless
 more animals in the future
 your unwanted furs may also help
 people in need because any coats
 they don't cover in fake blood for
 a demonstration PETA donate to

homeless people who can't afford
to buy their own coats
after all the homeless
are the only people
who have any excuse
for wearing fur
PETA have even shipped furs
to needy women and children
in sub-saharan africa]

it was nineteen eighty-four
i-i had money one icy night
i-i carried the greenham
common beaver fur coat
down the winding stair
from a high street flat
left it on the wintry kerb
by the wax museum
it was gone by morning
i-i make no excuse i-i cry
still bereft over the dead fur
of harmless herbivores
the futile tears of
reparative hairwash
i-i loved that coat
like a thrifted sister

it is october two thousand
and nineteen and bad surprises
are dropping like lemons
october's moon is the blood
moon or hunter's moon
say all the old almanacs
i-i say *is* is only the third
person singular present
indicative of the verb to be
and no one owns a moon
like no one owns a common
where all our want ladders start
pity the poor moon-given beaver
pity the poor beaver-given moon
we all know with gertrude it's hard
to write poetry in a late age when
the moon and the beaver and the coat
are not really there (some more absent
than others) when three thousand seven
hundred and fifty active nuclear warheads
are certainly somewhere and the very first poet
to land on a beaver moon is a brave dog
naomi littlebear molena the control tower
at greenham is now a community cafe
no you can't kill the spirit
but you can ruin it

with too much
lemonade

field animots

i-i like anything a word can do
i-i am a regular logophiliac
a word can do anything in a field
i-i like anything a field can do
my dog reg short for regimental
a poet of sorts soon at field edge spring heel
through the nose high corn hooked on rascal scent
yaps after stubble-stag jig foot hedge- squatter
earth-sitter light-foot fern-sitter kail-stag herb-
cropper creep-along sitter-still skiver
lurker faith-breaker baldy skull
and all the names of the hare
a dead naturalist can muster
go look them all up all seventy-
seven until its chief name (scoundrel) trembles
cornered at field corner
reg on three feet is all a-quiver
click of a zippo i-i drag deep
on a peter stuyvesant red
tasting the whole wide world
blue in a fume jagged nostril

same brand that killed my granddad according to
my dad who preferred to fur his arteries with

embassies number six he too took a dim

view of lagomorphia unless
by the hand of albrecht dürer
i-i see dürer's hand point to reg on three feet still
all a-quiver
i-i fume at this excess of lagomots i-i choke on
your access of lagopoeia in fact
i-i'm a lagopoeiaphobiac
yes a lagopoeiaphobiac
if one more hare is fielded
in this poem i-i swear to you you'll have me
screaming beware beware queen lapinova caught
in woolf's vicious allegory trap yes beware queen
lapinova
when all of a sudden
off the scoundrel fucks.

Harriet Tarlo

from CUT FLOWERS

writing a short poem forever

For Rachel Blau DuPlessis

they don't want anything because they
haven't got   *a brain* pushed
wild habitat   drifted long shore
in England   currents westward
thousands of   years, ice sheets
seeds   in easily erodible
particles   soft shingle ridges
dumped

sitting round the fire pit with Alice
casts   the sticks she
owns   she thinks she
a plant   owns a field
sprays   wipe out arable
flowers   seed edges resist
appear   from being
buried

no more wasted shots, choose one
stealing   to write from
to order   something more
prize   gets broken, little
so little   to be proud of
cry sheep   pasture too dry
look for   green in yellow
field

let your beard grow said the lady to
her friends   endless tea mugs
a flutter of   milk dugs a fluster of
children   single cell mosses
how do   they grow, chasing
they form   complicated patterns
green stage   forms against grass
lawn

that's the trouble with you, not a person
so much   stronger make to wait
subdue   adrenalin. Up. Back.
In. Stop.   Stay. Turn. I am ready.
sky   silhouettes, stationary
song   in tree tunnel, hear
felling   up & down volume of
fear

ring me as many times as you want
verges   date slots, windows
opposite   the old card shop
rows of   animals peeking at
up & over   each others' eyes
unlikely   coloured tails tired
to forget   unable to forget
an occasion

Rosie Roberts

a vacant formula

I was advised to come

upon arrival I notice each cupboard is stacked
with jarred goods:

iodine, chrysanthemum, birdseed, batteries etc

holding the film, the bell has rung out, culpable

I push back the door that swings heavily on
rusting hinges,

the street below is ploughed through to raw rock.

now diaphonus sheets ripple to the floor – the
notebook of an engineer of light, a diagrammatic
list of numbers pertaining to:

beams, shafts, dazzling spots and darkness.

Loose batteries have scared me since 1993.

A conflation of item, intention and horror

a layer of paper comes to lie over each place last
touched, bone dry and skin like, a memory of
flight.

other belongings – blue flecked detergent and
cumin were left around in small piles

if I took a deep breath and blew, the unaged Artex
would pick up a technicolour halo

must spilt onto the stage. An individual finds all
performances listed by title, and assumes they
are:

related, conventional, consecutive

They are foreign and unknowable.

Partial access; as an audience you inhabit *here*, **as forensic here,**

in *here* a regular home, and here a women's
tomb, coffee cups and ashtrays – poised

A played out past resonates, with interim
moments of unearthly labour. Insomnia is not
necessarily hereditary, so near them I hold my
breath, still feel somehow guilty

each room itself only
exists once then never again, repetition skirts the
Boarders of a perfectly mimicked knowledge
I hate my job. Philic and elitist.

An etching captured in dust on a heavy curtain
pencilled then there by a person:

'once there were piles of household goods here'.

Lila Matsumoto

A toppled valise emanated waves

A toppled valise emanated waves of inexplicable energy in the mathematical park. From its appearance I gathered it had been hastily abandoned and frozen overnight, and now its contents were splayed out before it like a nervous poker hand. A large and colourful towel intended for a faraway beach, an imitation toquilla hat. A paperback whose pages had rippled together, the title of which I was desperate to discover. As I poked at the book with a long branch, my dog's hackles began to rise, giving her body the appearance of an extended cockerel's comb. As if on cue, a child shrieked with uncurbed joy in the playground, plunging recklessly down the square root slide.

All of the pans in the kitchen

All of the pans in the kitchen were being used to
boil cauliflowers, submerging the house in a deep
mephitic funk. He showed me around, entirely
relaxed in attitude, lord of the duplex. A sort of
constant humming emanated from his body, even
as he spoke, producing curious and not entirely
unpleasant overtones. I had the strong impression
that he was an experimental ventriloquist. On top
of the dining table was a weightlifting bench,
because, he said, one should always exercise with
altitude. In the end I turned down the lodgings. I
couldn't imagine the musical group he insisted
we form, as housemates.

The dog wanted to go one way

The dog wanted to go one way and I, another.
The leaves pressed their five red fingers lightly
on the ground. All around us was casual
destruction, and I don't blame it on the weather.
Anyhow — we had gotten used to it, and made
jokes that felt like having your butt pinched by a
friend's partner. I admired the mien of the dog,
how in the distance her silhouette looked like a
fallen tree's, noble and tragic.

Colin Herd

Filthy Homes SOS

Ever google "famous tart tatins
of world literature" and then press
"Maps"?
Your poem / play...
What even is my type?
Start talking.
Jean Sénac
said "you are more beautiful than a self management
    committee."
My message is so watered down
I struggle to keep my head together
anything labelled "extra" I buy.
Do things the unintuitive counterintuitive
way around and turn them over
nothing could be simpler
and you get the sauce for free.
My back is spasming
all the boxing I've been doing
and lifting weights
improperly.
Money is the last thing anybody needs.
The Keto Diet.
A good blender.
I made this dessert that'll make you sick

in a loveheart tin with pears and blueberries
and cardamom.
Alexa is livid
not very clever
a honey wasp nest
I really like grating things
not your parent more accidental like
prestigious poetry magazines
and being able to speak about your feelings.
Whirring seems like the most
popular sound this year.
The tin was rubber
just the word extra
is enough
like a baby name
this fetish for authoritative voices
I miss being made
to look like a dipstick
one thing I've never felt
and I'm not complaining
is being pricked all over like
a potato.
Art is the same. Tinglestabs
to stop you exploding. When
am I going to learn?

Paul Hawkins

upside 4 d at moss (*?wot ru protektin m8*)

kapitalizts wnt hair spray
root ch-ch-ch-chAng
animL law
JNGL laws

trump's hair iz burdock
c%d b dandelion
johnson's horseradish
c%d b solomon's seal
root ch-ch-ch-chAng
somTIN somtings hapNn
putins cauliflower fungus
c%d b birch polypore

JNGL laws
plastik law
animL laws
wedr law

cle_n up fa_tor_s*et_ (riot nw)
art*sts b_*_*ets n_t p_an_s (riot nw)
_*_itor the oceans (riot nw)
c_i**weed th*_r gas t*nks (riot nw)
s**i_e The Clo*_ (riot nw)

it's ma ma ma ma marmalade manmade

still they want hairspray <period>
with or without you/i/we/they/them/those/ don't know scien-
    tists that disagree with that
use global warming on street corners
heat the homeless wash the homeless
bundle up bundle down
take the know-belle back from AI Gaw...
he wants us to clean up factories
artists brackets
turkey tail sky
cloud shrooms
plants to protect us from melting

if you eat more dock root milky oat seed kelp we'd be noncom-
    petitive in the manufacturing world stop laughing at US
    <stoopididdy> they want dark web hairspray right now

(Am) erika is champion cleanest clime

it's all upside for the at moss!
snort all shale enigma energy!
sniff all oleander resins!
snort fine wine soil reserves!
- **bear grylls**

based on stadistic stats
add up best it's getting better

we have ended the war on clean beautiful coal

begun negotiations to re-enter (i) the Paris-Dakar or (ii) a
    new transactional contrakt
on terms that are fair
to clean beautiful people
their businesses
porch-guns
chicken-fry spores
billionaire taxpayers
& homeland sec-sec sick-security

if drones spewed yarrow into the at moss
we made clean beautiful bullets with nettles
golf courses from calendula

take whatever survive means

say *don't use hair spray*
it's bad for the world erogenous zone
or they saying *use hairspray* <period>

nicky melville

Gaia Theory

Dear the Police

I would like to report some
thing that didn't look right
in the street
two potential terrorist axe

there were three girls
teenagers   maybe
fourteen or fifteen year old
(who can tell these days?)
they were laughing
showing some
thing or other
on their phones

I heard one of them
say   tell the truth
to a boy   who joined
        an obvious reference
        to Extinction Rebellion
        the movement
was all very
suspect

the clue's
in the name

it must be stopped

climate change in deed!

furthermore
there was a lamp post
and on that lamppos**t**
there were some stickers

and I t**h**ought I could make out
an hou**r** glass or **a**n **X**
but it is a while
since I had my eyes checked

and nearby   just along
was a wee old woman with
a dog

and when I passed
I thought I heard her
say 'climate emergency Gaia'

Gaia is a strange name

for a dog
I'm sure you'll agree
which pricked up my ears

if one wanted to give
the old dear the benefit
of the doubt
she could have said
'that was a bit of an emergency Gaia'
for there was indeed
a foul mess on the pavement
directly beside the dog

however   the proximity of both
groups to the sticker
makes one square the circle
or in this case   triangle

or does it?

maybe this is just
a load of fuss
about nothing

we'll never know
or *may*be

it is a hoax

terrorists don't kill people
poems do
here's a fucking poem
and it might kill you

we'll never know

until you start to froth
at the mouth
from the anthrax
on this paper
you fascist pigs!

Kat Sinclair

Voice II

Darling, when the rapture comes I want you to know that
it's okay to evangelise
it's okay to not
it's okay to want to be told it's okay
it's okay to not want to be told it's okay
everything is okay
it's okay that everything is okay,
okay? Let's begin.
Your father and I are separating –
he has taken a job as a rubber chicken tied to the front
of a removal van
and I am going to become a ball in the breakroom ball
pit
full time, this time.
When I got home I was high on pigeons
plump round droplets in lines look up forget that
hemorrhoid itch
when you were on your way to therapy
you saw: C's house, which had some cultural
appropriation in it
like weed smell, or exposed lightbulb in the bathroom;
Marine le Pen on the basement level window of a
seaside property
built as a Victorian summer home not to withstand the

salt whip;

a Dachshund, long;

moreishness, even longer;

the feeling of being late to the organising meeting (not
very organised, is it);

and a single Camel, unsmoked but wet.

Therapy was fine but on your way home you realised

you weren't sure if the bird bath was a war memorial or

if the war memorial was a bird bath

so you became weighed down with a deep oysterish
sadness

so addictive since you convinced yourself if you bear
down

in a squat, shell shut, you could produce something

to be worn around rich ladies' necks, the closest you'll
ever get

to literally becoming the guillotine

which would solve all your issues with alienation

as well as your deviated septum.

So you can see why we might want to leave

the digital tampon startup, or WiFi lights flashing on the
sanitary bin

you've been keeping us up all night

we never wanted a Smart Child

when we brought you into this Smart World

we never wanted you to be connected we just wanted

you to
learn how to cut an onion in the proper way so we could finally
leave you unsupervised
but I have become frightened of the washing machine
since the door won't open
my clothes have taken on a new, ominous wetness
shaking fibrous fists, trapped in plastic
just you try and wear me now
they scream, and they're right –
I wouldn't dare.
Make me proud, my little welfare state,
my endless marble run,
my novelty birthday candles which last forever
but only for a little while,
and darling, stay safe out there, where things flow –
like the world is a new hire and
we're the employee equity –
we've all been burned, our tiny matchstick legs,
money-mouthed, clove-eyed, lucky.

Nasim Luczaj

i am no tardigrade

these black
snowballs are
lava tripping
over itself
over and
over again

imagine if
one by one
we carried
every rock
down the volcano
as a souvenir
leaving a smooth
crater
fuming

as it is
there's
no entry
even for
sunstrangled grass

and i need some time

a whole life for instance
to process my luck

anticipating plastic

after The Garden of Earthly Delights
by Hieronymus Bosch

there are things i will always love
bosch for: product design

implying bouncy castle and bomb,
the smell of an unrequired armband,
alien mini golf; unmedieval material;
the waterpark where's-wallie-but-in-cgi
feel.

when i first saw the garden of earthly
delights irl i was wheeling my friend
round the prado, for she had broken
her leg playing catch, was ¼ plaster
cast.

this is how we got the best view,
parked right in front of the shoal
of cameras, the wall-large screen
capture of vicious bliss straight ahead
and on it more detail
than could be computable.

at least no devil in there –
unlike a number far-flung into infinity
he was not to be pinpointed,
only ever slithering off-axis
see-through and unaccountable,
being maybe the idea of an oil baron.

anyway we were fond
of the work being too complicated –
familiar in complication – a mouthful
with so many ulcers there were enough
for each to stand for a single glint
in a night's worth of a city lit
for going back to. we got to recycle
our delight in looking.

i found the word *synthetic*
in front of that garden
and mouthed it
as if it were the sheen of amen
combatting an evil
not even in the picture

then caught my flight:
sat swatted
as a painting

leaving the armrest down
and the window
blind open

Biographies

Contributors

Sascha Akhtar

Sascha Aurora Akhtar is a mystic and a poet, for real. Her performances channel the full body (of language) and beyond into a flare, with flair. Her poems chew and spew the necessary wisdoms. Lean in and listen' (Dr. Kimberly Campanello, Lecturer Creative Writing, Poet & Performer). Sascha is the author of 6 collections of poetry, one book of translations (2020) & a collection of short stories (2020).

Vahni Capildeo

Vahni Capildeo is a Trinidadian Scottish writer. Their recent books include *Odyssey Calling* (Sad Press, 2020), including a Windrush sequence for the Collections in Verse project, and *Skin Can Hold* (Carcanet, 2019; longlisted for the OCM Bocas Prize). Capildeo is Writer in Residence at the University of York.

Fred Carter

Fred Carter is a union activist, researcher, and poet living in Edinburgh, where he co-runs the reading series and occasional anti-press JUST NOT. Recent work has appeared in *amberflora, algia, erotoplasty, Tenebrae*, and *Academics Against Networking*. He is currently researching a PhD on linguistically innovative poetry and the environmental humanities.

Sarah Cave

Sarah Cave is a writer, editor and academic living in Cornwall. She is working toward a practice-based PhD on the Poetics of Prayer at Royal Holloway and her third full length poetry collection.

Miranda Cichy

Miranda Cichy is a poet and PhD candidate at the University of Glasgow, working with taxidermy specimens to tell narratives of contemporary bird extinction. She is editor of *skein*, a creative writing journal for Dumfries' Crichton Campus, and she was shortlisted for the 2019 Wigtown Poetry Prize Fresh Voice Award.

Gloria Dawson

Gloria Dawson lives in Glasgow, and says 'because you know the personal is the political, and the political is personal' at least twice a week. Sometimes there is no-one there to hear it. Writing can be found in *para.text*, *Poetry Wales*, *amberflora*, *Zarf*, and *circlusion* (2018) is available from Zarf Editions. New work from Fathomsun Press coming in 2020.

montenegro fisher

Adrian Fisher and Luna Montenegro are artists, poets and film-makers exploring ideas of transformation and collaboration. Experimenting at the borders between the politic and the poetic in a multispecies multi-verse. mmmmm.org.uk

Jane Goldman

Jane Goldman is Reader in English Literature at Glasgow University and likes anything a word can do. Her poems have been published in *Scree, Tender, Gutter, Blackbox Manifold, Adjacent Pineapple* and elsewhere. Her first slim volume is *Border Thoughts* (Leamington Books, 2014). She is preparing a new collection *SEKXPHRASTICS* for publication in 2020.

Jane Hartshorn

Jane Hartshorn is a poet based in London. Her practice explores the relationship between chronic illness and sexual identity. She has had poems published in *amberflora, para-text,* and *Front Horse*. Her pamphlet *Tract* was published in 2017 by Litmus Publishing. @jeahartshorn

Paul Hawkins

Paul Hawkins works mainly in poetry, visual art & performance. They co-run Hesterglock Press & its Prote(s)xt imprint with Sarer Scotthorne. They also curate events, run workshops, collaborate with & support SJ Fowler's Poem Brut project as a performer, artist & publisher. They've written a number of books, some collaborative, some not. The most recent is *Go Sift Omen* (Knives Forks and Spoons Press, 2019). Their work has been exhibited widely. KF&S Press will publish

EACHWHAT Vol.1, a Poem Brut-ish artwork this August. More info: eachwhat.com / hesterglock.net

Colin Herd

Colin Herd is a poet and Lecturer in Creative Writing at University of Glasgow. His books include *too ok* (Blazevox, 2011), *Glovebox* (Knives, Forks and Spoons, 2013), *Click and Collect* (Boiler House Press, 2017), *Swamp Kiss* (Red Ceilings Press, 2018) and *You Name It* (Dostoyevsky Wannabe, 2019).

Therese Keogh

Therese Keogh (b. Warrnambool, Australia) is an artist, living and working in London. Her practice explores the socio-political conditions and materialities of knowledge production, through narrative writing, studio-based experiments, and interdisciplinary fieldwork projects. Therese works collaboratively – through exhibitions, publishing, and teaching – across sculpture, landscape architecture, archaeology and geography.

Daisy Lafarge

Daisy Lafarge's first poetry collection, *Life Without Air*, and a novel, *Paul*, are forthcoming from Granta. She received an Eric Gregory Award in 2017 and a Betty Trask Award in 2019, and is currently working on *Lovebug* - a book about infection and affection - at the University of Glasgow.

Katy Lewis Hood

Katy Lewis Hood is a poet, editor, and PhD student from the East Midlands, currently living in East London. She co-edits the online eco-poetry magazine *amberflora*, and her poetry publications include *SWATCH* (glyph press, 2019) and *infra·structure* with Maria Sledmere (Broken Sleep Books, 2020).

Nasim Luczaj

Nasim Luczaj spends a lot of the time cornering bliss in Glasgow, where windows are large, ceilings are high, and puddles are portals. In between writing, translating, and screenshotting, she runs [underthunder] – a Subcity Radio show for weaving words into dance music – and DJs under the same name.

Francesca Lisette

Francesca Lisette is a poet, artist and diviner from south-east London. Their second book *sub rosa: The Book of Metaphysics* was published by Boiler House Press in 2018. As of Fall 2020, they will be a PhD candidate in Creative Writing & Literature at the University of Denver.

Lila Matsumoto

Lila Matsumoto is a poet and lecturer based in Nottingham. Her publications include *Urn & Drum* (Shearsman), *Soft Troika*

(If a Leaf Falls Press) and *Allegories from my kitchen* (Sad Press). Lila is one half of the poetry/music duo <u>Cloth</u> and co-runs the poetry journal/performance platform *Front Horse*.

nicky melville

nicky melville makes found, visual, process and experimental lyric poetry that interrogates the imperatives of language and ideology. His most recent book is *ABBODIES COLD : SPECTRE* (Sad Press, 2020). A natural pessimist he hopes to be proven wrong, but when he sees 'Final Days' on a sale poster for Peacock's he starts to wonder.

Iain Morrison

Iain Morrison is based in Edinburgh where he works as a live events curator in an art gallery. *I'm a Pretty Circler* (Vagabond Voices 2018) was shortlisted for the Saltire Poetry Award. Recently Iain's been reading 18th century travelogues by poets of their journeys through Scotland, Thomas Gray's being one example.

Timothy Morton

Timothy Morton is Rita Shea Guffey Chair in English at Rice University. He has collaborated with Björk, Laurie Anderson, Jennifer Walshe, Hrafnhildur Arnadottir, Sabrina Scott, Adam McKay, Jeff Bridges, Justin Guariglia, Olafur Eliasson, and Pharrell Williams. Morton co-wrote and appears in *Living in the Future's Past*, a 2018 film about global warming with Jeff Bridges. He is the author of the libretto for the opera *Time Time Time* by Jennifer Walshe. He is the author of *Being Ecological* (Penguin, 2018), *Humankind: Solidarity with Nonhuman People* (Verso, 2017), *Dark Ecology: For a Logic of Future Coexistence* (Columbia, 2016), *Nothing: Three Inquiries in Buddhism* (Chicago, 2015), *Hyperobjects: Philosophy and Ecology after the End of the World* (Minnesota, 2013), *Realist Magic: Objects, Ontology, Causality* (Open Humanities, 2013), *The Ecological Thought* (Harvard, 2010), *Ecology without Nature* (Harvard, 2007), 8 other books and 250 essays on philosophy, ecology, literature, music, art, architecture, design and food. Morton's work has been translated into 10 languages. In 2014 Morton gave the Wellek Lectures in Theory.

Max Parnell

Max Parnell is a writer, musician and translator of Brazilian Portuguese. His work has appeared in Adjacent Pineapple, SPAM, Gutter, Multifoco, Terramoto and Text Shop Experiments. His first novel, *Type I*, focuses on the ecologies of contemporary technology and is forthcoming with Dostoyevsky Wannabe.

Kashif Sharma-Patel

Kashif Sharma-Patel is a poet, writer and editor focusing on cultural history, racial aesthetics and queer performance across multiple forms. They are the co-founder and head editor at the 87 Press. Kashif has published and performed poetry across a number of platforms with a full-length collection *Dreaming Death* forthcoming. They also write music, art and literary criticism.

Pratyusha

Pratyusha is an Indo-Swiss writer and co-editor of the online literary journal *amberflora*. Her debut pamphlet *Night Waters* was published by Zarf Editions in 2018, and her pamphlet *Bulbul Calling* came out with Bitter Melon Press in May 2020.

Nat Raha

Nat Raha is a poet, activist and scholar living in Edinburgh, Scotland. Her poetry includes *of sirens, body & faultlines* (Boiler House Press, 2018), *countersonnets* (Contraband Books, 2013), and *Octet* (Veer Books, 2010). Nat holds a PhD in Creative & Critical Writing from the University of Sussex, UK, and co-edits *Radical Transfeminism* zine.

Rosie Roberts

Rosie Roberts (Glasgow) is an artist and writer interested in observing overlapping relations in the context of perceivable time. She focusses on paratextual matter, for instance: live presence in tandem with an artwork, footnotes as evidence of time spent reading; entwined events and (auto)biographies. Her practice is interdisciplinary and her work hybrid in form.

Calum Rodger

Calum Rodger is a Glasgow-based poet, critic and editor. Recent publications include *PORTS* (SPAM, 2019), *Rock, Star, North.* (Tapsalteerie, 2020) and, as editor, *Makar/Unmakar: Twelve Contemporary Poets in Scotland* (Tapsalteerie, 2019). These days he mainly likes to write about philosophy and videogames, which he shares at https://ontographicmetagaming.wordpress.com/

Mike Saunders

Mike Saunders is a library worker and trade union organiser based in Edinburgh. Publications include a chapbook about George Clooney, a documentary play about corporate manslaughter and airbnb, and the books *Dark Pool Ripple* and *Assynt*. He is currently writing about land, water, boredom, and the sun.

Kat Sinclair

Kat Sinclair is a doctoral student at the University of Sussex working on the political economy of feminised robots. She is the author of *Very Authentic Person* (The 87 Press) and *The Very Real Prospect* (Face Press and Earthbound Press).

fred spoliar

fred spoliar is a poet and education worker who lives in London and conducts errant research into Anthropocene aesthetics and the cultural history of waste. Their poems can be found in publications including *adjacent pineapple*, *datableed*, *mote* and *SPAM zine*.

Rebecca Tamás

Rebecca Tamás works as a Lecturer in Creative Writing at York St John University; and her poetry and criticism has been published in *The White Review*, *The London Review of Books*, and *Granta*, amongst others. She is the editor, with Sarah Shin, of *Spells: Occult Poetry for the 21st Century*, published by Ignota Books. Her first full length collection of poetry, *WITCH*, came out from Penned in the Margins in March 2019. It is a Poetry Book Society Spring Recommendation, and was chosen as a 'Poetry book of the Year,' in the *Guardian*, *The Paris Review* and the *Times*.

Alice Tarbuck

Alice Tarbuck is a poet living in Edinburgh. Her first pamphlet, *Grid*, was published by Sad Press 2018. Recent work appears in *Makar/Unmakar: Twelve Contemporary Scottish Poets* (Tapsalteerie). She is a 2019 Scottish Book Trust New Writer's Awardee for Poetry. She is part of 12, an Edinburgh women's poetry collective.

Harriet Tarlo

Harriet Tarlo is a poet and academic interested in place, landscape, environment and gender. Her poetry appears with Shearsman Books and her artists' books with Judith Tucker with Wild Pansy Press. She is Reader in Creative Writing at Sheffield Hallam University, U.K.

Samantha Walton

Samantha Walton's books include a collection of ecological lyrics *Self Heal* (Boiler House, 2018) and a pamphlet of omens for the anthropocene, *Bad Moon* (SPAM Press, 2020). She co-edits Sad Press, works at Bath Spa University and is based in Bristol.

Jay G Ying

Jay G Ying is a Chinese-Scottish writer and translator based in Edinburgh. He is the author of two pamphlets: *Wedding Beasts* (2019) and *Katabasis* (2020). He is a Contributing Editor at *The White Review* and Assistant Poetry Editor at *Asymptote*.

About the Editors

Maria Sledmere

Maria Sledmere is a DFA candidate in Creative Writing at the University of Glasgow. She is a member of A+E Collective, music journalist, editor at SPAM Press and Dostoyevsky Wannabe, founding editor of *Gilded Dirt* magazine and cohost of a podcast, *URL Sonata*, and workshop series, *Pop Matters*: a studio for thinking 'the alternative'. She has collaborated with artists including Lanark Artefax, Scott Crawford Morrison and North Sea Dialect, and performed at events such as No Matter, Queer Theory, The 87 Press, Just Not and the European Poetry Festival. Recent publications include *lana del rey playing at a stripclub* (Mermaid Motel, 2019), *nature sounds without nature sounds* (Sad Press, 2019), *Rainbow Arcadia* (Face Press, 2019), *Pure Sound*, with Max Parnell (SPAM Press, 2019), *Virga* (Earthbound Press, 2020) and *infra•structure*, with Katy Lewis Hood (Broken Sleep, 2020). Her poem 'Ariosos for Lavish Matter' was highly commended in the 2020 Forward Prize, and her work was included in *makar / unmakar* (Tapsalteerie, 2019), an anthology of contemporary poets in Scotland.

Rhian Williams

Rhian Williams is a stay-at-home mother and writer who lives in Glasgow. She is the author of *The Poetry Toolkit: The Essential Guide to Studying Poetry* (3rd edition, Bloomsbury, 2019), regularly reviews for SPAM zine, and has published many pieces on poetry and ecology over the last ten years. You can find her at: rhianwilliamswriting.com

Typographical Note

In attempting to respect the wishes of the contributors, this volume contains a range of typographical styles throughout (including pages 181-188 and 195-200).

Printed in Poland
by Amazon Fulfillment
Poland Sp. z o.o., Wrocław

85496920R00174